Vietnam Rising

The INDEPENDENT INSTITUTE

THE INDEPENDENT INSTITUTE is a non-profit, non-partisan, scholarly research and educational organization that sponsors comprehensive studies of the political economy of critical social and economic issues.

The politicization of decision-making in society has too often confined public debate to the narrow reconsideration of existing policies. Given the prevailing influence of partisan interests, little social innovation has occurred. In order to understand the nature of and possible solutions to major public issues, the Independent Institute adheres to the highest standards of independent inquiry, regardless of political or social biases and conventions. The resulting studies are widely distributed as books and other publications, and are publicly debated in numerous conference and media programs. Through this uncommon depth and clarity, the Independent Institute expands the frontiers of our knowledge, redefines the debate over public issues, and fosters new and effective directions for government reform.

Vietnam Rising
Culture and Change in Asia's Tiger Cub

William Ratliff

The INDEPENDENT INSTITUTE

Oakland, California

The Independent Institute
100 Swan Way, Oakland, CA 94621-1428
Telephone: 510-632-1366 · Fax: 510-568-6040
Email: info@independent.org
Website: www.independent.org

Cover Design: Christopher Chambers
Text Design and Composition by Leigh McLellan Design
Cover Photographs: ©iStockphoto.com/Pham Thi Lan Anh; ©iStockphoto.com/Serdar Yagci; ©iStockphoto.com/oneclearvision; ©iStockphoto.
com/Keith Molloy

Library of Congress Cataloging-in-Publication Data Available

ISBN-13: 978-1-59813-026-3 (pbk. : alk. paper)
ISBN-10: 1-59813-026-9 (pbk. : alk. paper)

10 9 8 7 6 5 4 3 2 1   08 09 10 11 12

Contents

Preface

AMERICANS OF MIDDLE AGE or older have "known" Vietnam for most of their lives, but until recently only as a Conradian "heart of darkness." And no wonder. From the rout of the French in 1954 to the ignominious flight of the last Americans from Saigon twenty-one years later, Vietnam increasingly consumed our lives in every way, as of course it did even more so the lives of the Vietnamese people. Critically important, on the American side, the Vietnam War was not fought by a volunteer, professional military force supplemented by private contractors, as in Iraq, but by draftees from across the nation. Almost three million Americans were sent to Vietnam during a fifteen-year period and fifteen times more Americans died there than have been killed so far in Iraq. Many Americans sometimes still think of Vietnam as a "code word" commentary on war and foreign policy, but with increasing frequency it is now thought of as what it is today, Asia's most recent economic semi-miracle or "tiger cub."

During much of the Vietnam War, I was teaching at Tunghai University in Taiwan and working on my doctorate in Chinese history. But the war and my studies of China very often turned my attention to Vietnam with its more than two millennia of Chinese influence. I didn't actually visit the country until early 1994, however, when I was lecturing on the first small cruise ship to visit Vietnam after President Bill Clinton lifted the 30-year trade embargo. We arrived at Da Nang early on a clear morning to a sight I will always remember: small, bobbing fishing boats a mile out at sea, on all sides of our ship, with one to several people aboard each of them waving flags and shouting "OK" or any other English expression they knew. Cynics would say they just wanted to sell us something, and no doubt some had families on shore that hoped to do so. But no one in the little boats had anything to sell, that I saw, and I received the greetings at sea and the welcomes by many others later on land as very genuine expressions of goodwill. In Da Nang, a few people, who had obviously worked for the Americans when we had a large base there, sidled up to me and asked, "Do you know So-and-so? I worked for him." Our guide to Hui spouted the official line about the alleged communist triumph in the 1968 Tet Offensive, until politely reminded in private of some facts. Then he said, "Ah, you know. Of course, you are right, the communists got clobbered," which was not just polite, but true. Already the Chu Chi tunnels outside of Saigon (which by then had already been renamed Ho Chi Minh City) were being turned into tourist attractions, though they have been spiffed up a lot since then. As the years have passed, I think almost all foreign visitors have found the Vietnamese similarly hospitable—whether they came as tourists, and of course bought some handicrafts from budding and industrious merchants or as investors, from Bill Gates on down. Some Vietnamese government officials and others probably think that U.S. and other foreign advisors are, in Gilbert's lines from *The Gondoliers,* "as plentiful as tabby cats, in point of fact too many," but the Vietnamese have often learned from (and sometimes rejected) much of what the visitors have to say.

While for many years I have averaged about two months annually in China, I have also continued periodic trips to Vietnam, as an academic, journalist, and tourist. I went to Vietnam, Laos, and Cambodia in 2006 as faculty lecturer on a Stanford University tour, and returned this year. Each time I visit the country I am more impressed by the spirit and dynamism of the people and by their determination to transform their lives and thus bring the long-embattled, stagnant, and repressed land into the modern world.

I am particularly struck by the influence of residual Chinese tradition in contemporary Vietnam, though it is largely unconscious and long-since adapted to Vietnam's history, conditions, and people. I call this influence "people's Confucianism," found throughout reforming East and Southeast Asia. It is the deeply ingrained Confucian, Buddhist, and Daoist traditions imported directly and indirectly over the millennia from China which continue to guide the thinking and actions in varying degrees of hundreds of millions of Asians in their daily lives. These qualities can be what Argentine Mariano Grondona calls "progress-prone" or "progress resistant," if progress means economic development and the wide-ranging benefits that follow. But Vietnamese life is also structured in part by the Imperial Confucianism that provided the code and tools of governance for both China and Vietnam for many centuries and that has its own "prone" and "resistant" qualities still seen and felt throughout Vietnam (and China) today.

Newspaper editorials I wrote after my Stanford visit led to two invitations to write in more detail on Vietnam's current conditions and future prospects. One came from Lawrence Harrison, director of the Cultural Change Institute at the Fletcher School (Tufts University), to examine in more detail than I do here the impact of traditional Chinese culture on Vietnam's recent economic reforms. Alvaro Vargas Llosa at the Independent Institute asked me to write on Vietnam for this series he is editing on global entrepreneurship, and this book is the result. Here I strive to put the reforms undertaken by the Vietnamese government and people since 1986 in the context of Vietnam's history and culture. Vietnam represents the most recent major Asian effort to transform a traditional society into a modern nation without sacrificing the essence or soul of the civilization. Recent years have shown that many Vietnamese are determined to build more rewarding lives for themselves and their families. The unanswered question is whether both the government and people want major change enough to set aside or greatly modify some of the persisting cultural and ideological traditions, or if they can find a way to reform the cultural characteristics that in the past impeded development into characteristics that can promote constructive change. Vietnam's future will depend on how the they work out these challenges.

William Ratliff
Ho Chi Minh City
October 10, 2008

Introduction

WHEN AMERICA'S creeping involvement in Southeast Asia began, more than a half century ago, most Americans had never even heard of Vietnam. By the time the U.S. military left in 1975, *Vietnam* had become a household word signifying tragedy, humiliation, or a feeling of "never again," depending on the perspective and/or message of the ordinary citizen, war veteran, activist, analyst, or politician. But now Vietnam, like Kipling's leopard, is changing its spots, or at least some of them. The country, which is almost as large as California with well over twice that state's population, now seems more comprehensible to many Americans because it seems to be becoming more "like us."

The current transformation of the old communist enemy began in 1986, when the Vietnam Communist Party (VCP) government in Hanoi launched its so-called renovation, or *doi moi,* program. But the very word *renovation,* not reform, never mind revolution, should give pause to those who think the Vietnamese will henceforth talk and act just like us.[1] The goal of renovating, or looking backward in order to fix something that has gone out of kilter, is one of many Confucian perspectives that are still critically important today in Vietnam. Confucianism has many qualities that have fit well into the modern world, but historically it has been a philosophy of dealing with the present and future by learning from and in some sense trying to return to an idealized past. In Vietnam today, VCP leaders insist that renovating means getting the country's socialism back on track, sometimes admitting that some of the early mistakes were made by none other than the much-revered Ho Chi Minh, the Father of the country, and his closest comrades. In reality, some of the market-oriented changes being made today, if they continue to move forward, are more revolutionary for Vietnam than anything Ho and his comrades ever dreamed of.

Vietnam has little historical experience with most of the ideas, institutions, objectives, and policies that have been discussed and, in varying degrees, implemented around the country over the past two decades, despite efforts to make them fit into the past. Thus, all reforms in Vietnam must first be seen in the context of belief systems, ideas, and practices that long predate—yet include—communism, reaching back more than two thousand years. This phenomenon of the lasting impact of long-extant cultures and institutions of the past is not unique to Vietnam or China (where it is also critical but usually ignored). It is also bedrock from Latin America to Russia to the Middle East, where traditional thinking and practices based on ancient cultures and institutions are not easily and quickly changed by preaching, reforms, or military invasion, and where such change is often resisted.[2]

Within Vietnam, much debate continues over the desirability and impact of the ideas and institutions associated with market reforms and open economies and political systems, and not only because these seem to necessitate modifying or replacing some traditional beliefs and practices. One must also consider the complexity of undertaking fundamental reforms in any very poor country and the fact that frequently even seemingly simple data are incomplete, unavailable, contradictory, or doctored to undermine or support any number of reforms or other agendas. Many faces of corruption and vested interests figure into this complexity, because many people, particularly those who today enjoy degrees of privilege at various levels of the society, have a stake, whether honorable or shady, in the past and present conditions. Sometimes these interests can become reconciled to change, but often they can't. Thus, besides inertia, these interests make trade-offs and power struggles inevitable.

Relatively free markets were important in parts of Vietnam before *doi moi*, especially in the southern city of Saigon, now renamed Ho Chi

Minh City, where decades ago the Cholon district was filled with private enterprises owned mainly by Vietnamese-Chinese. When the VCP unified the country in the mid-1970s, after the end of the war involving the United States, the doors of those private businesses were slammed shut and seemed closed forever. Now the same VCP, having learned a few things over the decades at the expense of the Vietnamese people, is encouraging assorted kinds of businesses and entrepreneurship that it had previously condemned. Thus, Vietnam's reformers today look to the country's past for ideas. They also look, usually without saying so, to the experience of China, which began its reforms a decade earlier than Vietnam did, as well as to much of the rest of the world, including most of the country's Southeast Asian neighbors. At the end of the day, Vietnam's surging if somewhat strangled private sector during the past two decades has been the main engine of unprecedented growth in a previously moribund national economy.

This study begins with a brief review of political and economic conditions in Vietnam as of mid-2008. The more detailed discussion that follows is broken into four sections. Part I surveys the cultural and historical experiences that provide the foundation for current reforms, touching on critical links to Confucian China, a century of French colonial control, and earlier programs of the VCP. The latter discussion begins with policies implemented immediately after control was established in the northern part of the country and covers the changes that followed "reunification" at the end of the Vietnam War and the introduction of the *doi moi* reforms just over two decades ago. The section concludes with a consideration of the importance of socialism throughout the communist period, including today. Part II broadly examines the types of changes underway today, ranging from legal and educational reforms to dealing with and reforming the dinosaurs left over from the recent past, most importantly the banks and the state-owned enterprises (SOEs). Part III focuses on entrepreneurship in Vietnam today, with discussions of varying forms of enterprises and the difficulty of getting accurate statistics. The main emphasis is on small and medium-sized enterprises (SMEs), but the discussion also considers household enterprises, women entrepreneurs, and the involvement of overseas Vietnamese. Part IV focuses on several important challenges for SMEs, above all the often not very business-friendly practices with respect to land use and funding/credit, concluding with a quick walk through the business registration process. Part V consists of concluding comments that seek to weave these threads together, assessing the change that has been accomplished and the remaining traditional and institutional challenges to a truly open entrepreneurial climate. The appendix remarks on the many faces of international involvement today in Vietnam's reforms.

Survey of Conditions in Vietnam to Mid-2008

ACCORDING TO Asian Development Bank figures, Vietnam's per capita gross domestic product (GDP) has grown from $98 in 1990 to $833 in 2007, which puts the country very near the $906 point at which, according to the World Bank, Vietnam will become a lower-middle-income country. Several decades ago, Vietnam was a stagnant, seemingly hopeless nation receiving $3 billion annually in military and economic aid from the Soviet Union. The money did little good because it was accompanied by mountains of very bad advice that led to or enforced intellectual, institutional, and physical obstacles to development. Most of Vietnam's anemic trade was with the similarly anemic Soviet bloc countries and expired with them. But even as that bloc was collapsing, Vietnamese leaders began to realize that they were slouching down a dead-end street and decided to follow a lead long since set by some of their neighbors. The result, as the *Economist* reported in a special issue on Vietnam published in April 2008, was that Vietnam transformed itself from a "basket case to a rice basket."

It is no wonder that post-1986 developments in Vietnam are hard for Americans to get right. Vietnamese themselves often are uncertain as to just what is going on today and where it will end, and the optimism of recent years began sliding down in mid-2008 with rising inflation. As the *Economist* reported, "Vietnam has become the darling of foreign investors and multinationals." Still, very much remains to be undone, redone, or reformed before Vietnam can expect to consolidate and expand its gains for the common good. A handful of international organizations annually evaluate the countries of the world with regard to what they and many in the West consider positive and negative aspects of the business environment and degrees of economic freedom that contribute to national development and globalization. The World Economic Forum's *2007–2008 Global Competitiveness Report,* for example, ranks Vietnam 68 among 131 countries; the *2008 Doing Business* report of the World Bank and the International Finance Organization puts Vietnam 91 among 178 nations in the ease of doing business; and the *2008 Index of Economic Freedom* published by the Heritage Foundation rates Vietnam 135 among 157 nations measured.

In 2007, the growth in Vietnam's GDP was about 8.5 percent, with an average growth of more than 7 percent over the past decade.[3] In July 2008 the Asian Development Bank lowered its estimate for GDP growth in 2008 to about 6.5 percent. Despite drought, avian flu, and livestock diseases, agricultural output increased slightly in 2007, and agriculture remained the majority employer in the country. Still, agriculture's percentage of the national economy continues a two-decade decline. The breakdown of the national GDP by percentage per sector in 2007, with a comparison to 1990, was: agriculture 20 percent (down from 38.7 percent in 1990); industry and construction 41.8 percent (up from 22.7 percent), of which manufacturing was 21.4 percent (up from 12.3 percent); and services 38.2 percent (down from 38.6 percent).

Vietnam joined the World Trade Organization (WTO) in January 2007, and in some respects that has accelerated changes across the economy, ranging from land reform and decollectivization to opening the agricultural and business sectors to market forces. Foreign direct investment (FDI) pledges between 1988 and 2007 were US$83.2 billion, just over half of which was realized. Pledges in 2006 came to $10 billion, and in 2007, after the country's entry into the WTO and Intel's decision in late 2006 to build a gigantic assembly plant in Hanoi, they were $21.3 billion, much of which came from Taiwan, Singapore, South Korea, and Japan. In the early months of 2008, investors pledged more than US$15 billion in 320 projects. The largest was $4.2 billion by the Canada-based

Asian Coast Development Ltd., followed by $2.69 billion from the British Virgin Islands.[4] Vietnamese investors have $1 billion in projects in 33 overseas countries, most of them in nearby in Southeast Asia.[5] Between 1993 and 2007, official development assistance (ODA) from donor governments and international institutions to Vietnam totaled $41.2 billion, about half of which was disbursed, with about half going to transportation, telecommunications, energy, and industry. These funds have low interest rates and long, sometimes flexible repayment periods, but they are loans and will in the end become a burden if not used effectively, which often they are not.

Although the VCP has opened this door to greater opportunity, the Vietnamese people themselves have made the newly presented opportunities pay off handsomely in many ways, not least in the small and medium-sized enterprises (SMEs) that are the chief motor of Vietnam's growth. In the process, a country that experienced chronic, centrally imposed food shortages for decades has greatly reduced the percentage of the population living in poverty, from over 70 percent in the mid-1980s to 14.7 percent in 2007.[6] And the World Bank's *Vietnam Development Report 2008* notes correctly that "moving out of farming jobs into self-employment, and especially into salaried jobs, has been one of the main avenues for poverty reduction in Vietnam," and that job creation has above all been in the private sector.[7] Current production is so great that Vietnam has become one of the world's leading exporters of coffee and rice, much of the latter shipped to Indonesia, Malaysia, and Cuba. Other key exports include tea, rubber, cashews, wood, and fish products, the latter including fish paste, frozen shrimp, cuttlefish, and octopus. Crude oil exports are the main source of foreign currency, bringing in 21.3 percent of total revenues in 2006, compared to 14.8 percent by the next highest export, textiles. Output of oil is declining, and so profits come from higher prices, not increasing production.

But a surge in foreign investments, on top of increasing infrastructure bottlenecks and shortages of skilled labor have contributed to by far the highest level of inflation in the past two decades. By August

2008 food prices had increased some 75% over a year earlier. Increasing consumption and growth in manufacturing contributed to surging imports of raw materials and intermediate goods, with imports exceeding exports at the end of 2007.

In addition, other old problems remained, including inadequate financing and credit opportunities for SMEs, complex and often discriminatory land acquisition policies, and widespread loss of time and effort spent wrestling with bureaucracies and trying to follow, evade, or adjudicate complex or unclear legal regulations that even judges and lawyers often do not understand or choose to follow, causing businesses and others to turn very often to mediation instead of the courts. The economic growth rate remained good despite the persistence of many as yet unreconstructed SOEs and banks that are characterized by low productivity and high inefficiency. The main process for reforming these enterprises is equitizing, that is, transforming them from state-owned operations into shareholding companies and then distributing shares to workers, management, and private foreign or domestic investors.

The Vietnam Development Forum published a handbook aimed at Japanese SMEs that might want to invest in Vietnam. As Vietnam's strengths it listed good workers, political stability, a rapidly improving FDI climate, a good location in East Asia, and a large population; the weaknesses included unstable policy and law, poor infrastructure, irregular business practices, corruption, lack of supporting industries, shortages of skilled engineers and middle-level managers, and possible negative impact of integration.[8]

PART I

Background

1

The Confucian Soul
of Vietnam

OVER THE PAST CENTURY, a few researchers have probed the role of Confucian tradition in the formation of Vietnamese culture and life. On the one hand, the ancestors of the majority Vietnamese people (the Kinh, who make up about 86 percent of the population) may have migrated to the country from Southern China millennia ago, though only 3 to 5 percent of the 85 million Vietnamese today are identified as ethnic Chinese. Beyond this ancestry, influences on Vietnam came from China's direct political and cultural control of Vietnam beginning in the second century BC, only a century after China's own unification, and continuing until Vietnam's formal independence in 939 AD. The main philosophical and religious influences involved were Confucianism, Daoism, and Buddhism, all of which were important in the formation of various aspects of the Vietnamese character. My focus here will be on the Confucian element because it generally had the greatest impact on the economic and social milieu and on general living conditions.

One of the very insightful writers in English to bring the critical encounter of the past, present, and future into the heart of his analyses of current Vietnamese developments is Pham Duy Nghia, the head of the Business Law Department of Vietnam National University in Hanoi. In a recent book chapter, he noted correctly that "[t]he enemy keeping Vietnam impoverished lies deep in the Vietnamese soul."[9] Even after Vietnam's independence a millennium ago, critical Chinese influence, adapted to Vietnam's own characteristics, continued and in many respects even increased, such that, as Nghia writes, "The traditional state of Vietnam, the recruitment of mandarins, and the organization of society as a whole, were based on Confucian values and examinations" right up to the expulsion of the French in 1954.[10] The Vietnamese legal expert continues, "To appreciate the current situation in Vietnam, one needs to look back to the past to understand the way in which the Vietnamese govern their society based on their beliefs and culture." This culture and the institutions that represent it in the day-to-day world both impede and promote the growth of and prospects for entrepreneurship that I focus on here.[11]

It should be noted that even the dominant form of Buddhism in Vietnam came in large part by way of China. It was the Mahayana version rather than the more ascetic Theravada that reached Laos and Cambodia and made them more withdrawn in social and business practice than the Vietnamese. The Confucianism that was planted in Vietnam during Chinese control included some despotic statecraft of Qin Dynasty legalism, which became central to Vietnamese as it was to Chinese history and governance. American Sinologist John K. Fairbank calls this mixture "imperial Confucianism," because it combines the Confucian philosophical system with an enforcement arm perfected by China's great unifier, Qin Shi Huang.[12] Or, as Nghia puts it, "Confucian values were newly underpinned by penal sanctions" and thereby "transformed into enforceable norms."[13] Thus, Vietnamese Confucianism was used to govern and control, only recently adapting in such a way as to help bring Vietnam, like China, into the modern, increasingly globalized world.

Historically, Confucianism developed interrelated traditions and institutions that had and still have an impact on life, reform, and entrepreneurship. These include:

Elite rule. Government is from the top down, a practice justified by philosophies developed through history that set hierarchies, relationships, and values with respect to individuals, families, society, and the country's leadership. Nationally, power was exercised by the emperor or dynastic head through a bureaucracy trained in Confucian moral values. The emperor's absolute power, exercised through his bureaucracy, was theoretically based on his having the Mandate of Heaven, which in practice he gained by inheriting or effectively seizing political power. Hierarchical relationships also prevailed within families, with the father filling the role of the emperor of his family, both in leadership and in maintaining links to the ancestors through proper rituals.

Morality. In Confucianism, moral values overwhelmingly trumped economic interests and goals, at least philosophically. Government leaders, from the emperor through the bureaucracy, were supposed to promote the people's interests and preserve harmony in society by providing leadership informed by moral training in the Confucian mold. The moral relationship was central also in the family. The bureaucracy, with its moral foundation, was selected through an examination system (and sometimes by other means) to bring moral leadership and harmony to society. Of course, some emperors and bureaucrats were guided to a certain degree by the perspectives of others, especially as dynasties began to wear down over the decades or centuries, and were motivated more by power, wealth, and profound moral and other forms of corruption.

Education. Education was highly regarded because it enabled one to perfect one's character for the betterment of one's self and society and, in practical terms, because it was the main route to the power, influence, and wealth that came from membership in the bureaucratic ruling elite. Confucian education focused on studies of ancient texts relating real and mythical historical experiences that were memorized and then interpreted and adapted to current governance. The educational process was long and difficult, involving many years of study and the passing of one or more examinations, depending upon the bureaucratic rank one sought. Although people at all levels of society realized the importance and consequences of education, most historically could not afford the money or time to attend schools or study privately and thus had little chance of becoming part of the elite. Such a path was, however, usually open to them and in some cases was used to rise from obscurity and poverty to power.

Confucianism's main failure in China, paralleled in Vietnam, was an inability to adapt to outside challenges and some forms of thought.

Even today, one of the main challenges faced by members of Confucian-oriented societies, with their regard for memorized tradition, is a failure to think outside the box. Although many important inventions over many centuries came from China, the focus on rote learning of moral lessons from ancient texts meant that in many respects Confucianism discouraged (when it did not actually punish) the innovative individual, in particular the imaginative entrepreneur. Of course, Marxism has been the dominant philosophy in recent decades, and its attitude toward entrepreneurship has been even more jaundiced than Confucianism's.

Predominance of the group. Fitting into the group or community was a supreme virtue in the Confucian tradition, as it is, at least theoretically, in communism. Individuals were conditioned not to meddle with the hierarchy, but to do what was expected of them according to their position. Education was the most acceptable way for an individual to take initiative that could open doors to greater influence, power, and wealth. (In practice, there were other, less education-oriented ways to rise in the government hierarchy, such as buying positions or using connections.) From the family to the nation, harmony, consensus, and loyalty were the ideals rather than competition and individual creativity. People often saw life as "eating bitterness" (as the Chinese put it), so they worked hard, saved for the inevitable tough times ahead, and didn't rock the boat.

Business at the bottom of the hierarchy. Entrepreneurs and merchants were at the bottom of the Confucian hierarchy. Still, some enterprises flourished, although they were always subject to government tolerance. Intervention by the central government, ranging from bribes to outright confiscation and execution of merchants who fell out of favor, was a constant possibility and threat. Nghia points out that Asian business schools, in the spirit of the traditional Chinese art of war, describe business as being similar to military combat and that "Japanese and Chinese engage in economic competition as though they are engaged in war."[14]

In recent decades, many features of Confucianism have been successfully adapted to the modern world and have proven to be true assets in the transformation of societies in ways that Confucius could not have imagined. As I have written elsewhere,

> The profound, lingering, in many ways largely positive legacy of Confucian culture is not always consciously present, but it is there among leaders and people and guides goals and actions in ways that are rarely equaled in Latin America or India. Key aspects are the belief that: (1) education is the expressway to success; (2) goals should be far higher than mere survival and pursued with single-minded diligence and a relentless work ethic; (3) merit should be sought and rewarded; and (4) frugality and focus must guide the expenditure of funds and energies.[15]

With particular reference to China, but equally applicable to Vietnam, the predictable result of much Confucianism led to the old quip that the only poor Chinese in the world are the ones who live in China. This is no longer true with respect to China or Vietnam. It remains to be seen how successfully the community orientation of thinking and governance can coexist with intellectually innovative and economically creative and thus potentially disruptive individuals and groups.[16]

2

Modern History
France, War, and Communism

IN THE MIDDLE OF the nineteenth century, France expanded its colonial empire to Vietnam, seizing the region and exercising power formally by maintaining the old Vietnamese imperial system, exploiting the people and the land for its own interests. France used the Vietnamese people primarily for physical labor or to staff lower levels of the governing bureaucracy. In the longer term, the French affected Vietnam's future in several ways. First, long before the colonial period, French Jesuit Alexandre de Rhodes devised the romanized script for the Vietnamese language that is in use today, though for its first two centuries the romanization was used largely by missionaries while Chinese characters remained the official language of the ruling Confucian bureaucracy. Second, some industrialization and urbanization emerged in the previously overwhelmingly agrarian economy. Third, aspects of French culture, particularly the language and architecture, made a clear impression on Vietnam and are still observed throughout the country today. And fourth, French colonialism and contacts with Europe sowed the seeds of colonialism's own defeat by spurring the growth of non-Confucian Vietnamese intellectuals and nationalism. Socialism and communism were among the philosophies learned by some young Vietnamese intellectuals. Among them was Ho Chi Minh, who was introduced to communism while studying in France, thus beginning his life work of driving the French (and Americans) out of Vietnam and reestablishing the country's independence.

The Japanese occupation of Vietnam during the Second World War further incited sentiments for independence among Vietnamese nationalists. With Japan's defeat in 1945, Ho declared Vietnam's independence, but the French refused to retire gracefully. Vietnam's new communists militarily humiliated and overthrew the French in 1954 at Dien Bien Phu, an obscure name that had the resonance then that Baghdad has today. By the end of 1960, Ho and his colleagues had established Soviet-inspired socialist socioeconomic structures in embryonic form. These were implemented all over the north of the country during the subsequent two decades of civil war involving the United States and several non-Vietnamese allies supporting the anticommunist south.

After the United States and the government of South Vietnam were defeated in 1975 and formal unity was reestablished in 1976, centralization was expanded throughout the country, with communist leaders seeking to punish rather than constructively integrate those who had been defeated in the civil war, as foreign correspondents and Vietnamese survivors have described.[17] Le Duan, who had succeeded Ho Chi Minh as Vietnam Communist Party (VCP) boss in 1969 on the latter's death, rejected the reforming current already underway in parts of Asia, though not yet in China, the latter then devouring itself in Mao Zedong's Cultural Revolution. By their own choice, Vietnamese leaders launched economic policies that, while not so vicious as those in China, nonetheless impoverished rather than developed their country and isolated Vietnam from most of its neighbors when it was not at war with them, as in China, or conducting its own colonial war and government, as in Cambodia.

Commenting on the policies implemented after reunification, Vietnamese historian Nguyen Khac Vien writes that "by the end of 1960, North Viet Nam, for the most part, equipped itself with at least in an embryonic form socialist socio-economic structures." As Vien wrote in his book, under the heading "Errors and Illusions," all organs of party and state, including the mass organizations of women, youth, and labor, were mobilized "with a great deal of commotion" in a campaign to change Vietnam by "liquidating as quickly as possible all forms of private, family and capitalist economic activity." While this hit all families and private businesses, it was directed most brutally against Chinese-Vietnamese entrepreneurs in Saigon, thus sending hundreds of thousands in that ethnic group to sea as "boat people," many of whom perished before finding a friendly shore. As private enterprise was crushed, peasants in the south were herded into agricultural cooperatives like those that already existed in the north. Big state farms were created to serve as vanguard units. The result of these reforms under Ho Chi Minh, Vien wrote, was "an enormous bureaucratic apparatus" run from the top that had nothing but contempt for and hostility toward any form of dissenting ideas. It utterly failed to serve the needs of the Vietnamese people or even the government, except for concentrating its despotic power.[18]

Le Duan and his comrades continued these policies, constructing the basic framework of the postwar government along traditional authoritarian lines, with institutions that often very conveniently dovetailed with even stricter communist ideas and practice. These included a proclaimed focus on community interests, as determined by the self-appointed ruling elite, whose moral authority was based on its having vanquished colonialism and on its allegedly scientific communist creed, this taking the place of the traditional Confucian Mandate of Heaven. The chosen policies, which included the silencing of all opposition, were exercised through legal and other institutions that often resembled traditional models that were clearly indebted to Qin Shi Huang.

Only when Le Duan died in 1986 did Vietnamese pragmatists begin the so-called *doi moi* renovation program, just as Chinese reforms had to wait for Mao's death in 1976. Even now, VCP leaders continue to speak of a transition to socialism, and many of the institutional structures established by Ho Chi Minh remain in place to a significant degree.

3

Doi Moi
Renovation and Reform

VIETNAM IS ONE of the last five countries in the world to have a single-party communist government, the other four being China, North Korea, Laos, and Cuba. Since 2001 the general secretary has been Nong Duc Manh, the first ethnic minority leader to hold that position. (Manh is rumored to be a natural son of Ho Chi Minh, though he denies it.) The prime minister is Nguyen Tan Dung. Major decision-making power resides in the VCP through its Politburo, Secretariat, and Central Committee, the latter ruling on major policies several times a year and at congresses held every five years, the most recent dating to April 2006. Government ministries remain highly bureaucratic and opaque, and implementation of policy, often through provincial governments that are even more bureaucratic and corrupt, suffers from this fact. As in China, the 493-member National Assembly, which meets biannually, is becoming more active, achieving a somewhat broader popular representation and a degree of transparency.

In many ways, the leaders of Vietnam's renovation have followed China's post-Mao lead in promoting substantial and comprehensive economic change, stabilizing and opening the economy, and increasing individual opportunity and personal initiative in economic areas while largely blocking substantive political reform. China began a decade earlier and has been somewhat more decisive in many of its market-oriented reforms, but Vietnam has also, with increasing momentum, promoted export-led economic growth funded to a large extent by foreign investment. With its official entry into the World Trade Organization (WTO) in January 2007, Vietnam has broken away from much of the stagnation and isolation imposed by the policies of Ho Chi Minh, Le Duan, and other early VCP leaders. The reforms caused deep ideological differences to emerge within the VCP leadership, particularly in early party congresses, slowing the reforms considerably during the period 1996 to 1999.[19] Having adopted and finally jettisoned much but not all of the disastrous Soviet economic model implemented decades earlier, and having their own party's survival in mind, VCP leaders have shown no significant interest in recent Russian or other European transition experiences that, through democratic elections, might eliminate single-party leadership.

The VCP has presided over the reversal of the stagnation caused in large part by its earlier policies, and it is quite successfully guiding the country into the modern world. Vietnam has become the newest seriously reforming Southeast Asian tiger cub; indeed, it is the star today among the region's older tigers. In recent years Vietnam has had the most consistent growth record of all the Southeast Asian nations, its GDP going from a low of 4.7 percent in 1999 to 7.8 percent in 2006, at an annual rate of growth averaging about 8 percent. This success was attested to in the VCP's Tenth Congress held in April 2006, when Nong Duc Manh, 56, was reelected party general secretary, while younger leaders were elected president (Nguyen Minh Triet) and prime minister (Nguyen Tan Dung). It was symbolic that several top party officials stepped out of party meetings long enough to grab a photo op with Bill Gates of Microsoft, the superstar capitalist and the world's richest man, who visited Hanoi at the invitation of the VCP, receiving pop-star acclaim.

Vietnam's economic growth has been driven by an increasingly market-oriented perspective that encourages private enterprise and a burgeoning private sector. Prime Minister Dung laid out the parameters of Vietnam's perspective when addressing an Asia-Pacific Economic Cooperation (APEC) finance ministers' meeting in September 2006. The Prime Minister said, "The Vietnamese government puts a high priority on macro-economic and public finance stability, and on that basis, promotes the roles of the private sector and development of the financial sector."

He added that Vietnam will continue to pursue its goal of achieving high and sustainable economic growth based on promoting industrialization and modernization, perfecting market economy institutions, developing a knowledge-based economy, encouraging education and training, and ensuring social justice. [20] The private sector has expanded by about 20 percent annually in recent years, has created hundreds of thousands of jobs, and has become the major force in substantially raising general living standards. During his visit, Gates himself urged Vietnam to move seriously into information-technology services and promised investments of his own in what he opined could become the next "miracle" in Asia. [21] On November 25, 2006, in the VCP daily *Nhan Dan,* Dung stated the "new strategic tasks" of "the trade sector together with the entire Party, army and people." They are: "accelerating economic growth, creating important breakthroughs in increasing development efficiency and sustainability, and to lift the country out of its underdeveloped status to become an industrial nation by 2020." [22]

Democratization is not on the VCP agenda. Nonetheless, the majority of the population seems to regard the VCP leadership as legitimate, both because the party led the way in throwing out colonialism and because it is now undertaking remarkably constructive economic reforms. [23] A small dissident movement advocating more Western-style democracy in the country is carefully watched and sometimes harassed, and as of now has no significant influence. A Vietnamese-American engineer in Silicon Valley, who was jailed for more than a month on his last visit to Vietnam in late 2006, says his recently formed People's Democratic Party has hundreds of members, 90 percent of them in Vietnam. [24] According to an official from Amnesty International, recent activities by democracy advocates seem to have contributed to a clampdown on Internet use, ironically just as the government was beginning to reduce restrictions on the Internet. [25]

4

Socialism

Nirvana or Not?

THE CURRENT SITUATION in Vietnam is more complicated than many analysts realize or seem prepared to acknowledge. Not long ago, many political leaders, academics, and ideologues in many countries worldwide based their ideas and policies on the assumption that socialism is the great destiny of mankind. Many others, of course, believed that even if self-professed socialist leaders are well-meaning, socialism as an economic doctrine is often nonsense. Many today, including numerous old Socialist True Believers, acknowledge that socialism, particularly the most hard-core communist forms, falls very far short of the ideal civilization Marx and his followers said was inevitable. From many reports in the Western media and from nongovernmental organizations (NGOs) and others on the spot, one might conclude that VCP leaders have accepted this negative judgment regarding socialism and have concluded that Vietnam needs only market forces, however difficult those may be to get started due to inertia and assorted interests on the ground. But this conclusion would be premature. Many VCP leaders and policy documents still speak of the transition to socialism as a roadmap to nirvana, while others doubtless regard it more as a dinosaur that they can't yet chase out of the backyard.

Note that the country is still called the *Socialist* Republic of Vietnam, though the 1992 constitution doesn't mention socialism very often, and when it does it seems unable to decide whether it is already here or still coming. For example, the preamble refers once to "the light of Marxism-Leninism" and twice to the current "transition to socialism," while other sections speak of the need for armed forces that will "safe-guard the socialist regime" (Article 45) or for "safeguarding socialist legality" (Article 132), as if the socialist regime and socialist legality already exist. It would not be unreasonable, considering the vanguard roles communist parties have always claimed for themselves, to suppose that the VCP means that the socialist foundations are indeed already here *in themselves and the party,* while the country and people as a whole are still making the transition toward the elevated level already occupied by the VCP.[26] At the same time, it should be added that some leaders and many Vietnamese people who consent to follow the rules set on high still look on all this with a jaundiced eye.

Note that the current reform program is called renovation, presumably because it is intended to get the country back on track toward socialism after several decades of false starts. The preamble to the 1992 constitution speaks of the current period of market-oriented production as a transition to socialism made necessary, as historian Vien explains, by the fact that Ho Chi Minh and Le Duan were indeed mistaken in thinking that "socioeconomic backwardness could be overcome by directly shifting to 'large-scale socialist production,' by skipping the stage of capitalist development." Still, the historian and others seem to maintain that their "illusion" was not in seeking socialism but in "thinking that . . . one could skip stages and push forward rapid development."[27]

The party position on socialism in the wake of the April 2006 congress was explained on the VCP website in an article entitled "Socialist Democracy—Goal and Motivation of Renovation." According to a professor at the Ho Chi Minh National Political Academy, "One of the most significant achievements of the 20 years of renovation in Vietnam is bringing into full play socialist democracy. Socialist democracy is associated with the Rule-of-Law State of the people, by the people and for the people under the leadership of the Communist Party"—using a phrase that Abraham Lincoln might consider out of context. He added that socialist democracy reflects "the superior nature of socialism," and continues, "To advance towards socialism together with development of a socialist-oriented market economy, acceleration [of] industrialization and modernization and construction of an advanced Vietnamese culture of strong national identities, it is imperative to successfully build socialist democracy, exercising great national unity, building the Rule-of-Law State while developing a pure and powerful party." [28]

Another clue to much current thinking is offered in another article in the *Communist Party of Vietnam Online Newspaper,* which states, "Proactive international economic integration is targeted at expanding markets, attracting more capital, technology and managerial expertise with a view to stepping up socialist-oriented industrialization and modernization and realizing a prosperous people, a strong country, and an equitable, democratic and civilized society." [29] Thus, there is considerable reason to believe that many party leaders do believe that market-type policies today will lead to some sort of "real socialism" in the future.

Questions remain nonetheless about this advocacy of socialism, the impact the "ism" has on VCP leaders, and indeed its ultimate viability, whatever party leaders may think about it. Even if VCP officials are sincere in their support for socialism, will it all be swept away in the end by the irresistible momentum of the market? Or do VCP leaders perhaps anticipate possible reversals in the reform process and want to be in a position to reestablish more authoritarian power to "defend socialism during its hour of crisis," as Fidel Castro has claimed to do in recent years, against the rising tide of market-oriented globalization? Or is continuing talk of socialism simply cynical manipulation of old traditional as well as communist paternalistic promises, now made by party hacks whose main motivation is their refusal to share power with others? Or is this an even more cynical effort by party bureaucrats to seemingly promote virtue while they arrange the seizure of assets for themselves, as, most famously, young Soviet communists did to become the billionaire oligarchs in contemporary Russia?

For now, I suggest that in most cases a socialist *orientation* is meant more seriously than cynically—though all the above-mentioned possibilities and others doubtless pass through many minds in Hanoi and especially Ho Chi Minh City, designating a tilt toward socialism in the sense of a degree of paternalism in policymaking and control. Paternalism is a central characteristic of both traditional Confucian and modern communist belief. And as Vien said, it is part of the historical process at this stage on Marx's escalator of history—the capitalist growth stage preceding the arrival of socialism and then communism.

PART II

Overview of Reforms Today

COMMUNIST PARTY LEADERS, at their April 2006 congress and on other occasions, sometimes sound more like disciples of Milton Friedman and F. A. Hayek than of Karl Marx and Ho Chi Minh, though they continue to speak and often think of reforms as ultimately serving socialism, as noted in the previous section. For now, at least, articles and editorials in the media and other publications promote ideas, legislation, and institutions intended to create an environment and rules of the game that will to varying degrees increase opportunities for entrepreneurship and economic growth. Committees, seminars, speeches, and publications are sponsored by the Vietnam Communist Party (VCP), foreign embassies, chambers of commerce, universities, and various international banks and other organizations.[30] Bill Gates was the most sought-after person in Vietnam during the week of the VCP's Tenth Congress. In this section I explore some of the ideas and activities promoted by these organizations and seen as influencing entrepreneurship in Vietnam. I then link these in the remainder of the study to, above all, small and medium-sized enterprises (SMEs).

5

The Legal Jungle

A KEY LONG-TERM FACTOR in the Vietnamese effort to create an environment encouraging the emergence and flourishing of entrepreneurship, particularly with the international dimension, is a legal system that protects domestic and foreign investors, their enterprises, profits, and persons. We should look first at Article 4 of the 1992 Constitution of the Socialist Republic of Vietnam, which states, "The Communist Party of Vietnam, the vanguard of the Vietnamese working class, the faithful representative of the rights and interests of the working class, the toiling people, and the whole nation, acting upon the Marxist-Leninist doctrine and Ho Chi Minh's thought, is the force leading the State and society. All Party organizations operate within the framework of the Constitution and the law." That won't make all investors entirely confident of impartiality.

The relationship between the party, national development, and the law is analyzed in a recent book entitled *Asian Socialism & Legal Change*.[31] The two editors write (p. 4) that "Vietnam is proactively seeking access to international capital and markets and has imported commercial laws and practices to secure these advantages." The lead author, John Gillespie, continues (p. 67) that above all in the commercial arena, "where the Party actively encouraged legal change, socialist legality has rapidly evolved in response to new economic ideas. Imported commercial laws are now beginning to supply the normative rules that were once almost exclusively the prerogative of Party edicts and moral campaigns."

In this context, several dozen laws and ordinances have been passed to comply with World Trade Organization (WTO) regulations, among them the Commercial Law, the Law on Intellectual Property Rights, the Common Investment Law, the Enterprise Law, and the Law on Competition. Among the laws passed in June 2006 was the Law on Lawyers, which contains new concepts for Vietnam, particularly rules on professional qualifications and legal practice, and articles on foreign lawyers and bars that will be permitted to operate in Vietnam.[32]

Turning to domestic law, the editors of *Asian Socialism & Legal Change* observe (p. 4) that "because imported legal reforms are not linked to underlying social processes, they are unlikely to engage with, and significantly alter, core socialist precepts like party leadership, democratic centralism and collective mastery." Thus, when preparing a revised Corporations Law, drafters were told (p. 9) "to take what was useful from capitalism while retaining socialist principles of state ownership and economic management." It follows that, as Gillespie adds (p. 67), "[c]hange is much slower where legal thinking impinges on Party and state power," citing as an example that "commentators discussing the capacity for socialist law to constrain Party political power are not permitted to consider Western 'rule of law.'" Looking to the future, the same author concludes (p. 68) that while in the commercial arena "imported laws interact and form hybrids with local norms and practices," this should not be expected for now in other social contexts "where political and moral discourses remain more powerful than legal discourse." There, "without compelling reasons to legalize or constitutionalise political processes, 'socialist law' is likely to remain faithful to longstanding Marxist-Leninist concepts."

In 1991 the Seventh Party Congress endorsed "state-based law." Just what this means is explained by Professor Hoang Chi Bao of the Ho Chi Minh National Political Academy. As quoted earlier, the professor wrote that "Socialist democracy is associated with the Rule-of-Law State of the people, by the people and for the people under the leadership of the Communist Party." Thus, analyst Elizabeth St. George (p. 119) concludes that "Socialist law in Vietnam is principally a set of instruments by which the state manages the country in accordance with the guidance of the [VCP]." The communist party is still above the law, except when the law is applied selectively against certain party members who are either excessively corrupt or in opposition to the policies of top leaders or both, as happens also in China.

The situation is further complicated by the way laws are written and implemented, or not implemented. Major laws are often passed six or so months before they take effect. Even six months later, however, the law usually is only formally in effect, and is not being implemented productively. As explained by Stoyan Tenev and colleagues, "New laws typically provide only a framework, leaving it to local governments to work out the details and resolve difficult matters" in enforcing the legislation. "Sublaws to guide the implementation are usually long in coming. Without guiding ministerial circulars, local bodies may be reluctant to move on a decree, even though it has already come into effect." Even when the administrative roles are clarified and inconsistencies in the legislation worked out, "there would still be substantial room for local authorities to apply their own interpretation to central policies."[33] These matters will be examined further in the discussion of the new Unified Enterprise Law, which was passed at the end of 2005 and took effect in July 2006, but for months had no supporting sublaws.

Broadly speaking, what is the result of these reforms? The rapidity and complexity of so much varied legislation has led to a great deal of inconsistency, contradictions, ambiguity, reluctance, refusal to enforce, and opportunity for what is diplomatically called "bureaucratic discretion." Legal procedures are frequently thwarted at the local level, leading a couple of provinces to set up a hotline that will put interested parties through to provincial officials for help. Pham Duy Nghia concludes his chapter on Confucian influences on Vietnamese law with the comment, "After decades of reform, the Vietnamese legal system today resembles a jungle of laws. It is evident that much has to be done if the mess is to be resolved."[34] Nghia further suggests that reforms were undertaken far too quickly and that Vietnam now must examine more carefully the reforms adopted after more careful study in Japan and Singapore. Gillespie and Nicholson believe (p. 13) that given Vietnam's "state-directed legal landscape," it is possible that "rather than promoting private legal rights, lawyers will prefer to mediate and negotiate their clients' interests with state authorities," even to the point of bribing bureaucrats and judges. This would be "entirely consistent with the situational and discretionary outcomes promoted by socialist legality." There is evidence that this is exactly what is happening, and it does not bode well for the smooth development of Vietnam's flourishing private enterprise at all levels of the economy.

Law schools in Vietnam are not in the vanguard of current reforms. Bui Thi Bich Lien (pp. 152–53), who began practicing law after a decade as lecturer at the Hanoi Law University, notes that "While state authorities and legal practitioners deal with market participants on a daily basis, law schools are still largely isolated from the process of economic and legal development. Legal academia," she continues, "remains an 'island' where socialist legal ideologies largely dominate. . . . Current curricula still lead law students to simplify the legal system according to the Soviet model and elevate the importance of state control, no longer appropriate in a diverse, market-oriented society." Law professors have recently been forbidden from working in the legal profession, and the vast majority of law graduates take jobs as state officials.

Thus, although aspects of the new legal system have been developed over the past two decades, the breadth of legislation and its implementation fall short of international standards or the ultimate requirements of a truly productive domestic business sector. An often useful study entitled *Doing Business in Vietnam* by the U.S. Commercial Service concludes that "Vietnam's legal system, including its dispute and claims settlement mechanisms, remains underdeveloped and ineffective in settling disputes," adding, however, that rather than the legal system itself, "negotiation between concerned parties is the most common and preferred means of dispute resolution." A fine report too narrowly entitled

Managing Capital Flows by Vo Tri Thanh and Pham Chi Quang for the Asian Development Bank (ADB) Institute concludes that when it comes to foreign direct investment (FDI) in particular, "major obstacles . . . still exist such as red tape and corruption, an inconsistent and barely transparent system of legal documents and unpredictable policy changes." I discuss individual laws, planned or in place, in the sections that follow.

6

The Educational Tangle

COMING FROM a Confucian tradition, Vietnamese culture in general has long had a high regard for education. A report to the VCP's Tenth Congress in 2006 focused on the critical role of education and training when it stated that an important national goal is to "lay the foundations for accelerating industrialization, modernization and development of knowledge economy."[35] Still, despite considerable emphasis on education by the government since 1986, and the significant progress that has been made, a great deal more must be done to expand availability and quality to meet the nation's rapidly increasing needs.

Vietnam's expenditures on education are roughly average for the region, being higher than those of Indonesia and India, not to mention neighboring Laos and Cambodia, for example, but lower than the expenditures in Thailand and Malaysia.[36] The share of gross domestic product (GDP) spent on education has been rising steadily, reaching 4.6 percent in 2004, with a goal of 6 percent by 2010. The primary focus of the government's payments is basic education. The literacy rate is a bit above 90 percent and is slightly higher for men than women. Nationwide, levels of education remain very uneven, however, and are particularly low in rural and mountain areas and among the more than 50 ethnic minorities.[37]

The Vietnamese educational system is divided into the following layers: (1) compulsory primary for five years and (2) lower basic secondary for four years, followed by (3) either upper secondary or vocational and technical education, each for three years. Higher education (4) consists of college (3 years) or university (4 to 6 years). Already about 45 percent of children under six years of age have access to kindergarten, a number that is being pushed up slowly year by year. The World Bank reports that more than 98 percent of primary school–aged children are in class, though the United Nations says a significant number drop out of primary and secondary classes. The main reason for dropouts at the upper level, it suggests, is a lack of money to pay fees, but another is peer pressure on boys, suggesting that respect for education does not always survive adolescent growing pains and that "boys will be boys" even in a traditionally Confucian society.

One result of the *doi moi* program has been the privatization of some education. There are very few nonpublic schools at the elementary level, where education is compulsory and free. Rather, the private schools are concentrated at nonelementary levels. Nonpublic schools must abide by the same laws as the public schools with respect to everything from curriculum to teaching, testing, and diplomas.[38]

Very specialized education is available in some places, with or without a university degree, but still in small amounts. There are high-quality foreign high schools such as the Australian and British International Schools, which are expensive but are attended by many Vietnamese as well as expatriates. An insightful study by the Vietnam Development Forum, a joint Vietnamese and Japanese project, entitled *Vietnam as an Emerging Industrial Country,* notes and lists some excellent industrial training programs, several set up in cooperation with Japan, Germany, and Singapore, but adds that they are far too few.[39]

The specialized education ranges from classes and seminars on international competition, intellectual property rights, tariffs, and how to invest in the stock market to information technology and community healthcare programs.

Intel needs some four thousand workers for its new chip assembly and manufacturing facility, scheduled to open in Ho Chi Minh City in 2009. Reportedly, most of these positions will be taken by recent college graduates, many from Vietnamese universities. Top students will be sent abroad for training before assignment to management positions in Vietnam.[40]

At all levels, however, education is in many respects falling far short of national needs. An American adviser to the Vietnamese Ministry of Education noted in mid-2008 that in equality of access Vietnam rates among the best in the world, but that the quality of the education leaves much to be desired.[41] For some years, and at an accelerating level, school graduates have not been well enough prepared for the jobs becoming available. *Thanh Nien News* reported on September 1, 2006, that Vietnamese graduates "in general lack communication skills, experience, and practical knowledge and so have to be retrained to be employed." Only 37% of graduates even get jobs after graduation.[42] Former Vice President Nguyen Thi Binh wrote in *Thanh Nien News* on August 23, 2006, that Vietnam must begin to draw investors for the *quality* of Vietnam's workers, not just their low salaries.

The problems go beyond curriculum to include inadequate facilities, pedagogical matters such as memorization and parroted responses, and overcrowded classrooms and schools. Schools often focus on learning by rote, with outdated, boring, and flawed curricula. Good colleges, universities, and vocational schools are essential for Vietnam's modernization plans, and the government has sought to get foreign universities to build Vietnamese campuses, despite the medieval stipulation that they have to teach Ho Chi Minh Thought. This can lead to complications, as in the case of Harvard University's Fulbright Economics Teaching Program, funded largely by the U.S. State Department, which teaches market ideas and Socratic pedagogy that were almost unheard of in Vietnam when classes began a decade ago. Harvard's objective was to teach and work with local institutions in promoting dialogue about substantial education reform in the country.

Often teachers are badly trained, and textbooks are filled with mistakes. A *Thanh Nien News* columnist wrote on July 21, 2006, that Vietnam's education system has been decimated by fake certificates and diplomas and that there is rampant cheating in many places. A rash of scandals in 2006, ranging from administrators' pocketing of money to exam fraud, has also tarnished the system. It was found that some parents were expected to pay bribes to get their children into good schools.[43]

A critical problem among university graduates is the gap between their academic knowledge and their practical knowledge, which has immediate repercussions in the business community. Universities and institutes have lacked close linkages with the business world, training quality and efficiency have been poor, teaching and learning methods are out of date, resources have been limited, and resource utilization has been inefficient. A review of provincial governance and competitiveness published in early 2008 concludes,

> Creation of a skilled labor force trails only land allocation in terms of urgency for future local economic development. According to the 2007 PCI [Provincial Competitiveness Index], nearly half of all businesses surveyed were unsatisfied with the quality of vocational training and other supporting labor services. Firms indicated that vocational training schools and centers are state-owned and apply obsolete curricula, which often do not offer courses in line with practical demands of the business community. These schools have neither the budget nor the incentive to upgrade services. Private firms (most of whom are small businesses) simply do not have the resources to train their employees. And even when the firms invest in training, they do so at the risk of having their employee poached by other businesses—particularly by those located in provinces close to major cities.[44]

There are constant complaints and pleas from businesses for better-educated workers, from laborers to CEOs. The salaries of the few qualified managers and professionals are sky-high. A reporter for the U.S. *Chronicle of Higher Education* concludes that "Vietnam's higher-education system is in a time warp: 20, even 30 years out of date." She adds that Vietnam "lacks a credible research environment, produces few PhDs, and is locked in Soviet-style pedagogy," with students still studying the "evils of capitalism."[45] Canon, the world's largest laser-printer company, tried to manufacture parts in Vietnam but decided to go elsewhere because the work quality was too low. The plant Intel is building in Hanoi will only assemble and test chipsets because, as the general manager of construction, Rick Howarth, said, Vietnam cannot now produce enough trained personnel "to meet the needs of the high-tech industry." Summing up the problems with Vietnamese education, he continued, "Their curriculum is antiquated. Their teaching methods are very hierarchical, meaning it's all memorization and passing test, vs. the practical application we're looking for."[46] Finally there has been too little institutional autonomy and accountability.[47]

Many foreign firms say that despite ridiculous requirements, Vietnamese workers are diligent, disciplined, and eager to learn. In 2004–5 some 230 colleges and universities and 122 postgraduate training units had nearly 1,350,000 students. This amounted to 140 students per 10,000 Vietnamese and was an increase of nearly 30 percent in three years. In May 2008 the Education Ministry reportedly set a target of 200 students for every 10,000 people by 2010 and 450 per 10,000 by 2020. A major problem, however, is qualified faculty. There were not nearly enough trained teachers for the 69 universities and 28 colleges that opened between 2006 and 2008.[48] A top government official said at the end of November 2006 that a general guideline handed down by the National Assembly states that the government will strive to speed up the establishment of private universities and hopes to place 40 percent of students in them in the future.

In the end, as a scholar with the Harvard Vietnam Economics Program said in a personal email, Vietnam's higher education is "highly dysfunctional." The Vietnamese Ministry of Education still requires degree courses to include antiquated fields of study, but those in themselves are "but one symptom of the failures of the system and the leadership and vision vacuum that plague Vietnam's reform effort. Problems that pervade the entire higher education system range from a lack of autonomy, to disincentives to innovate, to promotion not based on merit, to academic corruption, etc." Harvard experiences in Vietnam, while highly productive in important respects, suggest that "unless the fundamental issues are addressed, Vietnam will not be able to grow the skilled labor force it needs to realize its growth prospects." [49]

7

Monetary Policy
and Banking Reform

MONETARY POLICY WAS for many years the bane of
VCP leadership. Since *doi moi* began, the party has become more adept
in macroeconomic terms, though inflation is often too high and the
2007–8 period was an obvious backslide. Most in mid-2008 believe
the problem will be dealt with in 2009, though a Hong Kong–based
analyst with Morgan Stanley warned that Vietnam might be headed
toward a "currency crisis" similar to the catastrophic Thai baht crisis in
1997. In the end, much of the problem is the VCP's often unaccount-
able and arbitrary allotment of funds to ideological (or personal) projects, such as bailing out the state-owned enterprises (SOEs). In 2006 the
government moved ahead with a multiyear roadmap for reforming
the seriously flawed banking sector.

The failure of Soviet-era monetary policies was undeniable by 1986
when, as noted earlier, inflation that had been rising rapidly peaked at
500 percent or more. By the end of that decade increasing efforts were being made to reduce the negative consequences of the government's mar-
riage of politics and economics, particularly the incestuous economic
relationship between SOEs and the banks, which, though diminished,
continues to this day. Vietnam emerged stronger than ever from the
Asian crisis of 1997–98, and in terms of GDP growth Vietnam, though
little more than a tiger cub, began outperforming the more established
but temporarily wounded neighborhood tigers. Still, inflation has remained a concern and has forced national leaders to focus attention
on the importance of macroeconomic stability in relation to continued

rapid economic growth. Inflation fell to about 3 percent in 2003, rose to about 8 percent in 2006, and shot up to nearly 20 percent between mid-2007 and mid-2008. The government seems prepared to accept single-digit inflation so long as it does not exceed GDP growth.

Much bank reform has been underway in recent years, and progressively fewer problems originating in the Soviet and early reform periods remain. As one study notes, "In the initial stages of economic transition, banks were mainly serving as government windows to channel resources to SOEs."[50] In 1988, Vietnam formed a two-tier banking system with the State Bank of Vietnam (SBV) assuming central banking responsibilities with four state-owned commercial banks (SOCBs) to undertake commercial banking, then as now handing a significant amount of money to the SOEs. WTO membership dictated additional reforms, and by mid-2008 there were 75 banks in the country. In addition to the SBV, there were the Vietnam Social Policy Bank, five SOCBs, 34 joint stock commercial banks (JSCBs), 31 wholly owned branches of foreign banks, and other institutions. Some JSCBs and foreign institutions have built strategic partnerships in recent years. A 2008 report by the Asian Development Bank (ADB) Institute stated, "In recent years, the banking industry has significantly developed its financial strength by cleaning up banks' balance sheets and increasing capital through issuing new stocks as well as increasing financial reserves. As a result, the financial position of banks has been improved significantly in terms of capital adequacy and non-performing loans (NPLs)." The same report later elaborates, however, that although concerns about NPLs have gone down significantly, "the sustainability of loan quality is seriously questionable in the future." And "Viet Nam's banking system is still vulnerable due to limited supervision, monitoring and governance capacity. On-site . . . supervision is constrained due to inadequate quantity and quality of human resources."[51] The ADB Institute reported that the SBV is now "undergoing more radical reforms to be a modern, relatively independent central bank."

All SOCBs are now in the process of, or are lined up for, equitization, that is, selling off some of their shares so that they will be partially privatized. When the IMF recommended in about 2000 that one state commercial bank be equitized, government officials were willing to proceed only with the Mekong Housing Bank. A banking sector reform plan, aiming at and beyond the SOCBs, was adopted in 2001. The decision to equitize all SOCBs came quite quickly thereafter—much more quickly than action—while support for the key role of the state remained strong. For now at least, the government will retain a minimum of 51 to 80 percent of any equitized bank stock. After long delays, in December 2007 the Bank for Foreign Trade of Vietnam (Vietcom-Bank) finally made its initial public offering on the domestic market, and the Mekong Housing Bank is expected to do so next. The SBV has been directed to draft equitization plans for the Bank for Investment and Development of Vietnam (BIDV), the Industrial and Commercial Bank of Vietnam (Incombank), and the Bank for Agriculture and Rural Development (Agribank). In October 2006 VietcomBank followed the lead of the Vietnam Ministry of Finance and signed a deal to secure Microsoft's Office 2003 software, thus simultaneously guaranteeing use of more up-to-date technology and striking a blow for honoring intellectual property rights, which often does not happen.

Some U.S. and other international specialists have said that Vietnam's banking *legislation* often measures up to acceptable international standards but that its *implementation* is burdened by the leftovers of traditional and communist traditions and a local lack of expertise and/or foot-dragging. The repayment rate of credits appears strong, in part because so many loans are rescheduled. In fact, there isn't much choice: Seizing collateral is difficult in practice, and often the only practical alternative, even for well-motivated banks, is to reschedule. Overall, Vietnam remains a cash-based society, with more money stashed in homes than deposited in banks, though the banking sector has been expanding by about 20 percent annually since the beginning of the decade.

8

Resurrecting
the SOE Dinosaurs

AT PRESENT, one of the most costly leftovers of Ho's socialist misadventure still hangs on, namely the state-owned enterprises. The SOEs were first formed in the north after independence from the French, based on a Soviet model. When the communists took power in the north, they were doubly wrong in their use of the land, for they created communes on the agricultural side and passed out large areas of land to the SOEs. With the end of the civil war and unification in the mid-1970s, some 1,500 private enterprises in the south were taken over and converted into 650 more SOEs. In their heyday, these enterprises numbered well over ten thousand and, like the SOEs in China, were, together with the communes, a major part of the economy, largely because little else was allowed. They were usually highly inefficient, underproductive, overstaffed, and operating in the red. Again, like their Chinese counterparts, most of them to varying degrees drained the state banks via nonperforming loans (NPLs), which were frequently simple welfare handouts to "workers" who often did little or no work in an overstaffed and inefficient SOE.

When *doi moi* began in 1986, a key challenge was (and in many ways still is) the attitudes toward and practice of centralization as seen in the SOEs. It is embedded in many Vietnamese minds and institutions, the latter a product of the foreign communist influence. Here as in other areas, the question today is, to what degree have leaders changed their minds enough on matters of state control to seriously implement deep reform? In a long and often very critical report on SOEs published early in the millennium, Tran Ngoc Phuong, standing vice chairman of Ho Chi Minh City's Enterprise Reform and Management Board, reported that a 1998 study concluded that among SOEs, some "40% were profitable, 40% fluctuated around the break-even point and 20% incurred chronic losses." In 2000, just before an extra push was launched to equitize the SOEs, the percentages in those three categories were 40 percent, 31 percent, and 29 percent, showing an almost 10 percent slide in the "break even" and "chronic loss" categories. In mid-2008, according to the Ministry of Finance, there were 1,900 SOEs, about 600 of which are losing money and another 430 that have a "low earning ratio." [52]

Still, Phuong concluded that:

> The ten-year goals are to complete SOEs reform, enhance efficiency and competitiveness of SOEs to enable them to make important contributions to ensuring critical public services and social products as well as meeting the crucial needs of national security and defense. At the same time, SOEs must become the driving force of economic growth and serve as the foundation for industrialization and modernization along the Socialist line. [53]

In April 2008 Deputy Prime Minister Nguyen Sinh Hung reiterated this point when he told a national conference in Hanoi that it is important for the restructuring and equitization of SOEs to continue to guarantee that they will remain at the core of the national economy. [54]

There is no question that the SOEs continue to play major positive and negative roles in Vietnam. An ADB report in early 2007 noted that "the SOE sector in Viet Nam is a key pillar of the country's economy and a critical element to its continued economic growth. SOEs account for over a third of the country's GDP, roughly half of its exports, and contribute about 70% of the Government's tax revenue (i.e., in the form of VAT and Corporate Income Tax)." The government has also reported that SOEs hold up to 80 percent of credit capital from domestic banks and 70 percent of foreign borrowing capital, though their earnings are only 40 percent of GDP. The ADB concludes that "the sector is relatively inefficient. Overstaffing, very low corporate governance standards, inadequate accounting and reporting, poor oversight, and a lack of management expertise have been typical characteristics of the sector."[55]

Thus, the government is trying to substantially resurrect these socialist dinosaurs in a new and more efficient form, through equitizing them into limited or joint stock companies, often with a foreign investor but still controlled indirectly by the state. The pilot program began very slowly in 1992 and was pushed ahead slightly in 1996. Equitizing was speeded up with the opening of the Vietnam Stock Exchange in 2000. Between 2000 and early 2008, the number of equitized SOEs jumped to about four thousand, almost all of them small- and medium-sized, one of the few exceptions being the large Vietcombank in 2007. A majority of firms listed in stock markets in 2008 are SOEs that have undergone partial privatization or equitization. Beginning with Vietcombank in December 2007, the government in 2008–9 plans to conduct initial public offerings of a number of large SOEs. As in most cases in Vietnam, statistics are often contradictory, though the trajectory is clear, albeit moving by fits and starts. According to Pham Viet Muon, deputy head of the Steering Board for SOE Renovation and Development, 2007 saw 271 SOEs restructured and 150 equitized, bringing to 5,366 and 3,756, respectively, the numbers restructured and equitized in all.[56] According to the Steering Board for Business Renewal and Development, during the period 2007–10 some 1,553 businesses will be rearranged and 950 equitized, balancing the benefits of the state, investors, workers, and businesses.[57] By 2010 only 554 SOEs will remain fully under government control in the fields of national security, defense, essential public utilities, and agro-forestry.

In May 2008, however, an ADB Institute discussion paper reported that there were about 2,100 SOEs remaining, of which 1,500 have been or will be equitized by 2010. The paper noted, "The reform process is becoming more complicated as it touches the production factor markets and the large SOEs, which are socio-economic sensitive and related to the concept of socialist orientation."[58]

The privatization process sagged for the year before mid-2008, in part because of a stock market slump but also because of inefficiency, excessive administrative formalities, lack of coordination, and bad debts.[59] The state-owned Industrial and Commercial Bank of Vietnam (Vietinbank) reportedly will sell a 25 percent stake to domestic and foreign investors in an initial public offering by the end of 2008, with an additional sale of 24 percent by 2010, leaving the state with a 51 percent holding. In May 2008 the Vietnamese Ministry of Finance announced that all SOEs that are run ineffectively or make low (or no) profits, except those in the finance, banking, insurance, and securities sectors, will be put under ministry supervision.[60] Nguyen Duc Kien reported that a survey of 850 equitized SOEs in 2006 showed that 85 percent had become successful in production and business.[61]

Still, if the point of equitization is to make the SOEs more efficient and profitable, there are some unfavorable signals to note. That process alone won't do it, because many managers are political appointees from years past whose salaries and jobs are not dependent on good performance. The past suggests that it will be essential to get far more substantial stock in the hands of outside investors, who will then have to insist upon much more hard-nosed management and bookkeeping than is being exhibited by the leaders of so many equitized SOEs today. It was reported to the National Assembly Standing Committee in September 2006 that no equitized firm has ever hired an outsider as managing director and that the state's majority share in the equitized SOEs means no shareholder plays a role in the company's management.[62] Thus, the continuing problem of the state's role is exacerbated by the overwhelming number of old-timers in the leadership of the new companies. Reportedly, more than 80 percent of the original directors of the SOEs continue to hold their positions. Since the equitizing began, managers and workers have had first access to shares, and by the time they had taken what they wanted, in a sort of insider privatization, there was little left for outsiders. In 2003, some 52 percent of equitized SOEs sold nothing to outsiders, while by 2005, as some larger enterprises went on the block, outside participation had increased somewhat.

In addition, the number of SOEs equitized does not tell the whole story, for while the percentage of equitized SOEs is quite high, most of the enterprises involved were small or medium in size, their total chartered capital in early 2007 accounting for only 12 percent of the total state capital in SOEs.

PART III

Entrepreneurship in Its Several Forms

9

Introducing Entrepreneurship

WHAT FACTORS ARE most conducive to successful economic reform in poor and developing countries, or in any country for that matter? A critical element in the productive chain in Vietnam, as elsewhere, will be entrepreneurship. But how does one promote or enable productive entrepreneurship? Do people even want it? We can begin with the *Oxford Concise Dictionary* definition of entrepreneur as a person who is in effective control of a business or enterprise with a chance of profit or loss. One may continue that historical experience demonstrates a critical interrelationship between beliefs, policies, and institutions. The wrong combination brings inertia or disaster, while the right combination can lead to the creation of a free and secure environment that promotes entrepreneurship and innovations that, even when they fail, are themselves building blocks for further productive innovation. Two analysts concluded in the *Cato Journal* that "Because entrepreneurial activity tends to be the underlying factor that attracts more venture capital to an area, economic development policies should focus on creating an environment attractive to individual entrepreneurs, rather than on attracting venture capital." [63] Vietnamese leaders have made a fairly serious but still inadequate effort to encourage or just allow innovation. Millions of Vietnamese who were and are desperate to improve their lives have taken their chances by trying to open a business, even though the environment is still very far from ideal. Much foreign investment has come in over the years, most of it since Vietnam joined the World Trade Organization (WTO).

There are differing and overlapping perspectives on what makes up that ideal environment. In *Economic Freedom of the World,* the authors argue that the "key ingredients of economic freedom" are "personal choice, voluntary exchange coordinated by markets, freedom to enter and compete in markets, and protection of persons and their property from aggression by others." [64] On a different level, the World Bank lists the four steps to successful reform in Vietnam. First, "start simple and consider administrative reforms that don't need legislative changes." Second, "cut unnecessary procedures, reducing the number of bureaucrats entrepreneurs interact with." Third, "introduce standard application forms and publish as much regulatory information as possible." Finally, remember that "many of the frustrations for businesses come from how regulations are administered. The Internet alleviates these frustrations without changing the spirit of the regulation." [65]

Although the *doi moi* reforms of 1986 led to foreign investment and the creation of private businesses, a mass of complications discouraged many would-be entrepreneurs. These complications were reduced with the 1999–2000 Enterprise Law, which significantly simplified the labyrinthine registration and operation process for businesses. The results were evident as Vietnam became one of the fastest-growing economies in the world. A new Unified Enterprise Law took effect in July 2006 and will be discussed later. A lot has been accomplished with these reforms and laws. Still, for all the good news, serious impediments to rapid private-sector growth remain in the soul and circumstances of Vietnam, mainly cultural, attitudinal, and institutional leftovers from the recent and distant past. We will now look at the reforms that have been attempted and at some of what remains to be done if Vietnam is to achieve its objective of permanently leaving the underdeveloped world.

10

Enterprises in Vietnam
Legislation and Statistics

DURING THE just over two decades that private enterprise has been permitted in Vietnam, there has been an explosive
growth in microbusinesses or household businesses, as well as in small
and medium-sized enterprises (SMEs). The *Economist* stated, on April
24, 2008, that "Perhaps the most dynamic sector of the economy is
made up by the Vietnamese-owned private firms that have come from
nowhere since being legally recognized. The country's latent entre-
preneurialism has burst back into life." An International Monetary
Fund report in December 2007 noted that the private sector "now
accounts for more than 60% of GDP [and] has been the engine for
Vietnam's rapid economic growth and job creation."[66] Large-scale private enterprises are still uncommon in Vietnam, for reasons that will
be discussed in more detail later. Increasingly, the two most important contributors to the rapid reduction of general poverty across the
country have been household businesses and SMEs. Still, while the
growth in microbusinesses and the registration of SMEs have been
impressive, the Mekong Private Sector Development Facility (MPDF)
is correct to warn that some evidence suggests that the private sector
may not be as robust as the headline numbers (for example, the number of reported business registrations) might imply.[67]

Household Businesses

By far the most common form of private enterprise in Vietnam, emerging over the two decades since the government opened the door to private entrepreneurship, is the microbusiness or household business.[68] These microbusinesses have played a critical role in the lives of millions of Vietnamese. They have made it possible for people to earn at least meager incomes and to rise to some degree out of poverty caused by historical underdevelopment, wars, and earlier policies of VCP governments.

The two main surveys covering these types of business are both by Vietnam's General Statistics Office (GSO), but they use very different criteria and reach different conclusions. The *Non-Farm Individual Business Establishment Survey,* which defines a business establishment fairly precisely, reported 2,913,907 household businesses in 2004 and 3,053,011 in 2005. In contrast, the *Vietnam Household Living Standards Survey,*[69] the most recent of which dates to 2004, presents what the World Bank describes as "an exhaustive account of all non-farm self-employment activities, regardless of how insignificant they may be."[70] According to these criteria, Vietnam had 9.3 million non-farm enterprises run by households. This employment may be a primary, secondary, or even tertiary activity. The number has declined slightly since 1993, probably because wage employment has expanded from 16 percent to 27 percent during the same period. That is, although about 30 percent of Vietnam's employment was in household businesses in 1993, by 2004 it had fallen to 25 percent.

It is important to emphasize that these household businesses are informal in that they are not registered under the original Enterprise Law, though they may be listed with local governments. Although in 2001 these informal businesses occasionally employed up to fifty people, by 2003 almost no informal business did so. The most popular household industries involve commerce, accounting for about 40 percent of the total, and processing and manufacturing, about 25 percent. Almost 56 percent in 2004 were run or managed by women, a fact I discuss in more detail later, up from 49 percent in 1993, and these businesses in 2004 were more consistently profitable and professional than those run by men.

Why do so many household businesses choose to remain informal? The *Markets & Development Bulletin* of October 2005 expanded upon the factors. (1) The local environment and opportunities. Some provinces and cities are much more open to formal businesses, the most receptive being Ho Chi Minh City, which as Saigon had extensive experience in private enterprise before the VCP took over. (2) The size of the enterprise, including how many workers it has and the capital investment. (3) How successful the industry has been and what its prospects are for competing in a broader marketplace. Some industries are simply more widely salable than others, and thus formality makes more sense. (4) The background and training of the entrepreneur and his or her contacts in the outside world. (5) Whether the local infrastructure make outside markets accessible. (6) Informality lends itself to greater discretion on the part of tax officials but fewer regulations for the business. In late 2007 a professor at the Central Institute of Economic Management gave a seminar reporting that many household businesses don't want to change their business format because of cumbersome procedures in accounting papers and taxes.[71]

11

Private Enterprise in
the Broader Business Picture

The Progression of Legislation

THROUGH A SERIES of legislative actions beginning
with *doi moi,* Vietnam has enabled the emergence of a critically important private sector. The main way stations on this journey toward the
market have been the Foreign Direct Investment Law, which dated
from the time of the seminal VCP Congress in 1986, followed by the
Private Enterprise Law and the Company Law of 1990, which allowed
individuals to set up a business so long as they complied with a number of government regulations. Another major step was the official recognition of the role of private enterprise in Vietnamese development
incorporated into the Constitution of 1992, although that document
also reaffirmed the leading role of the VCP in laying out the direction and details of the country's future development. The Domestic
Investment Promotion Law of 1994 was revised in 1998 and opened the
Vietnamese economy to foreign investors.

By far the most important legislation was the Enterprise Law, passed
in 1999 and taking effect in 2000, and its successor, the Unified Enterprise Law of 2005, which officially took effect in July 2006. The 2000
legislation allowed Vietnamese to form businesses with a significantly
reduced level of government involvement, primarily by simplifying the
labyrinthine registration procedures considerably. The result was a leap
in the number of registrations. According to the *Business Issues Bulletin*
of August 2006, for example, 160,000 new firms registered during the

five years ending in December 2005, about three times as many as had registered in the previous decade, bringing the total number to more than 200,000.[72] The Asian Development Bank, in its *Asian Development Outlook 2006,* also spoke of 200,000 businesses. As I argue later, however, the data are in many respects not reliable. Even before the promulgation of the Unified Enterprise Law of 2005, the MPDF emphasized the need to go beyond passing legislation to the point of implementing it effectively so as to improve rather than complicate the business environment and effectiveness.[73]

The Challenge of Statistics, Again

This brings us back to one of the critical problems in trying to evaluate private enterprises and their role in Vietnam—namely, knowing with any degree of certainty how many there are, what their status is, and what they are up to. The challenge of statistics is evident in the case of the microbusinesses, the unregistered household enterprises. But the challenge in the case of SMEs is even greater and is critical in weighing the roles, indeed the existence, of formally registered enterprises. Two organizations are chiefly responsible for collecting basic data, and what they report varies widely. They are the National Business Information Center (NBIC) and the General Statistics Office (GSO).

The main activity of the NBIC is recording new company registrations, which it does through the provincial and municipal offices of the Department of Planning and Investment (DPI). These are the figures cited earlier that seem to demonstrate an explosive growth in private enterprises in Vietnam. They are available in real time or shortly after registrations have occurred. In reality, however, although the growth in the number of enterprises has been impressive, it is not nearly as explosive as NBIC figures seem to suggest, for many reasons. For example, as one MPDF study noted, drawing an analogy from population studies, "nearly all company births (and some re-births) are being counted in Vietnam, but most company deaths are not." It is very complicated to go out of business formally, and thus most that fail shut their doors and let it go at that. Other problems with interpreting statistics regarding new business registrations are that some existing firms tend to reregister several times, some firms register subsidiaries and branches in different locations as if they were separate firms, and some long-established household enterprises suddenly appear as new firms when they formally register. Other firms register but never really do much. These problems can occur in any country, but for our purposes they pose a significant problem in understanding the degree and vitality of growth.[74] Specifically, while NBIC-based reports of registered private businesses operating in Vietnam toward the end of 2006 suggest a number somewhere between 200,000 and 250,000, the GSO reported just 105,569 actually in operation at the end of 2005, a number that is probably much more reliable.

The GSO does not report as often as the NBIC; indeed, its figures are often at least a year old. It depends in large part on tax codes issued to each company by the tax department, and presumably these records come far closer to tallying the companies actually in operation. Thus, its report is entitled, in part, *The **Real*** [emphasis added] *Situation of Enterprises.*[75] In May 2005 the MPDF concluded that "there is roughly a 40% margin of difference between the NBIC and GSO statistics (and this margin is increasing every year)."[76] Indeed, by the time of the December 2006 GSO report, the margin with respect to SMEs had increased to 50 percent or more.

Thus, while both the NBIC and the GSO produce useful data when used carefully, the reports of the former are generally more misleading than helpful when discussing the vitality of private enterprises in Vietnam and should be cited only with the utmost care until at least some of its most serious problems can be resolved. Certainly the Vietnamese government should not discuss its policies and goals in terms of NBIC statistics.

12

Businesses in Vietnam

IN 2001 the World Values Survey of the Institute of Human Studies concluded that the Vietnamese are even more business oriented than the Chinese, though respondents in both countries, with their paternalistic cultural history, are more sympathetic to government involvement in business than people in more firmly established market economies.[77] The evidence of the Vietnamese proclivity for private enterprise is found in the growth of private businesses in the two decades. The most recent and probably most accurate (if dated) data are reported in the GSO's document entitled *The Real Situation of Enterprises Through the Preliminary Results of Survey Conducted in 2006*. The data, collected during 2006, seek to tally the enterprises actually in operation as of the end of December 2005. Although they are the best available, even these figures are undoubtedly more suggestive than precise.[78]

According to the GSO, there were 113,352 enterprises in Vietnam as of December 31, 2005, up 23.5 percent from the year before. Of these, some 105,569 were non-state, Vietnamese-owned enterprises, up from 35,000 in 2000; 4,086 were Vietnamese state-owned enterprises (SOEs), down from 5,759 in 2000; and 3,697 were foreign investment capital enterprises (FIEs), up from 1,525 in 2000, with slightly more than three-quarters of them fully foreign owned. The total number of enterprises increased by 28 percent annually after 2001, an average of 14,213 added each year, but declined in 2008 due to government policies.

Broken down by the focus of the businesses, some 42 percent were commerce, 22.5 percent were industry, and 13.5 percent were construction. Other areas, all smaller than 5 percent, included agriculture/forestry/fishing and restaurants/hotels. SOEs were most widely represented in industry, construction, commerce, and agriculture/forestry/fishing. The FIEs predominated in oil and gas.

Collectively the enterprises contributed 53 percent of the country's gross domestic product (GDP), though efficiency was low and even declined during the year. Return on equity for 2005 was 4.42 percent, compared to 4.85 percent in 2004.

In terms of numbers of employees, the average per SOE was up, from 363 in 2000 to 499 in 2005; the average number of employees in the SMEs was 30 people in 2000 and 32 in 2005. Among SMEs, 51.3 percent had fewer than 10 employees, some 44 percent had from 10 to 200 employees, and less than 2 percent had from 200 to 300 employees.

In terms of capital, the average for SOEs has risen from US$8,300,000 in 2000 to $22,700,000 in 2005, while the average for SMEs rose from $192,000 in 2000 to $447,000 in 2005. The capital investments in SMEs can be further broken down as follows: 41.8 percent were valued at less than US$64,000, some 37 percent were valued at between $64,000 and $319,000, and just over 8 percent were valued at between $319,000 and $639,000.

Foreign Invested Enterprises

One important form of enterprise in Vietnam today that falls largely outside the parameters of the current study is the foreign invested enterprise, which, like the privately owned Vietnamese businesses, were made possible by *doi moi.* Even prior to the beginning of the renovation program, VCP leaders had looked around themselves in Southeast Asia and seen the positive consequences of opening the nation to foreign investment. Thus, one of the VCP's first actions in 1986 was promulgating a Law on Foreign Investment, and enterprises arising as a result of that and subsequent legislation have played an important role in the development of the country and SMEs. Indeed, the Common Investment Law, passed in late 2005 and taking effect in July 2006, alongside the Unified Enterprise Law, is testimony to the continuing and even expanding Vietnamese interest in tapping resources from outside the country, as is the long-sought membership in the WTO, which occurred in 2007.

According to GSO reports, Asian capital has predominated in the FIEs, though a significant amount of that came from U.S. subsidiaries based in Asia. Early investments were often in construction or in such projects as hotels, offices, and infrastructure. More recently, the focus has shifted to transportation, communication, finance, and particularly to oil and gas exploration. FIEs are responsible for a major portion of the oil and gas production (almost 100 percent) and automobile assembly (84 percent) and for lesser but significant percentages in electronics, textiles and garments, chemicals, steel, cement, rubber, plastics, and food and beverages (between 25 and 45 percent). Originally these were joint ventures, usually with an SOE partner, since they were the only enterprises that could partner with foreigners. Since 1997 it has been possible to partner with private enterprises. Fully owned foreign enterprises now account for almost half of committed FDI capital in Vietnam.[79]

The main focus here, however, is Vietnamese enterprises that are entirely or largely independent of foreign investment, ranging from household businesses to the major group contributing so much to the current economy, the SMEs.

Small and Medium-Sized Enterprises

When considering the impact of the small and medium-sized enterprises, it is essential to recall that Vietnam is a very young society, with 60 to 70 percent of its people under 30 years of age. Roughly 1.5 million young Vietnamese (ages 14 to 25) join the work force each year, and most of them, according to a study by UNESCO and the Vietnam Ministry of Health, are reasonably satisfied with their jobs. The study shows that more than half of the new workers have simple, usually non-skilled, jobs. About a third, mainly in the urban areas, are self-employed, while a fifth work in household businesses, a tenth have salaried jobs in the private sector, and 7 percent work for an SOE. Considering the job creation experience of Vietnam in recent years, the *Vietnam Development Report 2006* concludes that only the domestic private sector is in a position to massively create jobs in an affordable way. Experiences to mid-2008 confirm that judgment.[80]

The government and some in the SME world reportedly have a goal of 500,000 businesses in operation by 2010, which would be a major challenge even if NBIC figures were reliable. If the GSO figures are roughly correct, with an average of 14,213 new businesses being added each year to the current total of 113,352, it would take well over a quarter century to arrive at 500,000. At an SME roundtable in Hanoi in December 2007, the vice chairman of the Vietnam Chamber of Commerce said that *50,000* new businesses had registered during the year, and he again forecasted 500,000 by the end of the decade.[81] Despite these projections, the president of the Vietnam Chamber of Commerce and Industry, Vu Tien Loc, lamented that no detailed plans or strategy have been designed to accomplish this growth.[82]

Even if the goal of 500,000 businesses were reached, an official in the Vietnam Economic Institute noted that there will still be only six businesses for every 1,000 people, in contrast to forty-nine for the same number of people in Taiwan. On the other hand, remember that household enterprises, some of them of significant size, are far more numerous than the formally registered businesses tallied in NBIC and GSO reports.

The Enterprise Law of 2000 left many complications and a playing field that was still, in important ways, hostile to private enterprise. As the *Business Issues Bulletin,* published by the International Finance Corporation's Mekong Private Sector Development Facility (MPDF), reported in June 2005, private firms could not participate in big state-funded projects or compete internationally because of their small size and limited capacities. In addition, access to land and premises was limited, investment capital was insufficient, and in some areas regulations restricted rather than facilitated development, especially on tax issues. The *Bulletin* reported that the tax calculation and administrative system, including VAT invoice controls, seriously impeded transparency and thus access to capital and other inputs needed to support firm growth.[83]

The Unified Enterprise Law was drawn up in response to problems with the 2000 legislation and changing conditions in the country and internationally. Wisely, it was written over a several-year period in consultation with different groups in society, a consultative approach that has been practiced for many years by the reforming tigers of Southeast Asia. (The broader Socio-Economic Development Plan 2006–2010 was also drawn up with the participation of the government, large organizations, academics, the private sector, civil society, and development partners.) The new Unified Enterprise Law is supposed to help create a more equal, transparent, and open investment environment for Vietnamese and foreigners; further simplify registration procedures; and reorganize the basic types of enterprises, though it does not do so in all of the problematic areas noted earlier. What is more, as the *Business Issues Bulletin* of October 2006 reported, the business community continues to be concerned that, as is often the case in Vietnam, the practical implementation of laws and decrees can be inconsistent with the laws themselves.[84] As is true with so much Vietnamese legislation, repeated drafts of the essential implementation decrees, giving guidance on what the laws mean, did not begin coming out until six months after the law. Many ambiguities remain because of uncertainties with regard to meaning and implementation and, indeed, due to continuing inadequacy in the law itself in many respects, despite improvements. The October 2007 *Business Issues Bulletin* stated that recent legal reforms were "particularly noteworthy" in the areas of investor protection and access to finance, although the World Bank's *Doing Business 2008* report gave Vietnam low marks for "protecting investors," ranking it 165 out of 178 countries, while for "getting credit" Vietnam ranked 48 of 178.[85]

Women Entrepreneurs

Vietnam has a generally good record among developing nations in promoting gender equality, a record that dates back several centuries. Education and health levels are roughly similar for men and women, although according to the Vietnam Women Enterprise Council, women currently own only about 20 percent of the registered businesses in Vietnam. They run a higher percentage of the household businesses. In the *Business Issues Bulletin* of April 2006, Trang Nguyen, the manager of the MPDF's Business Enabling Environment Program, noted that women represent 52 percent of the work force and own about 30 percent of the businesses.[86] A study of firms varying in size from 137 to 17,543 employees found that 80 percent of workers in the dynamic garment and footwear industries are female; most are young, single migrants with an average monthly salary considerably higher than the minimum wage. Indeed, most of the workers in the industries, male and female, are reasonably satisfied with their jobs, and women in particular consider the garment and footwear industries as ways to escape from farming. The larger firms were foreign and joint ventures, while the smaller ones were private enterprises and even SOEs.

The MPDF has produced two excellent studies of women entrepreneurs in Vietnam, one published just before and one after the VCP's Tenth Congress in April 2006.[87] Some of the conclusions reached apply to SME problems generally, but many are directed toward the challenges faced by women specifically. The government has officially committed to gender equality, and women frequently say that their problems are due not so much to discrimination, though that is sometimes present, but to influence.

Voices of Vietnamese Women Entrepreneurs, an MPDF examination of 473 businesswomen, focuses, often in considerable detail, on the following frequently closely interrelated needs and concerns of women entrepreneurs: (1) The legal guarantees as they apply to women are usually well intended but are still evolving and inconsistent. For example, women often have particular trouble proving that they own land, in large part because women's names are often left off critically important Land-Use Right Certificates. As a result, among other things, collateral is not officially available and access to credit is greatly complicated. (2) Women have common concerns, sometimes the same as men's, sometimes different, regarding the difficulty of finding capital and managing finances. (3) Since much business is conducted somewhat informally and through connections, women find doors to government officials and clients harder to open. This is often because women, particularly younger women, are not taken seriously, as the *Economist* remarked, until they have more than proven themselves. Thus, women want associations and networking opportunities that are tuned to and discuss their specific needs, where they can exchange ideas and experiences. (4) Like men, women have a day-to-day need to expand markets and find and retain qualified staff. (5) Finally, women face the special and inevitable problem of reconciling the demands resulting from being wives and mothers as well as businesspeople.

In the end, the women in *Voices of Vietnamese Women Entrepreneurs* expressed a clear need for (1) training in entrepreneurship and assorted business instruction directed specifically toward women with their special challenges and styles; (2) improved access to land and finance, addressing in particular but not solely the challenges faced by women; and (3) an official channel of access by means of which they can relay their needs to policymakers.

A study in late 2007 by Danida, the Danish Development Assistance organization, showed that providing support for female entrepreneurs was a way to improve employee benefits in SMEs. The report demonstrated that female firm owners are more likely to provide benefits regardless of educational level, firm size and age, legal ownership, location, or sector.[88] Women are the main force behind many small-scale banking and aid programs, ranging from the Grameen Bank to small private enterprises in Vietnam's less-developed neighbors.

Overseas Vietnamese Involvement

According to the Committee for Overseas Vietnamese, some 3.5 million Vietnamese currently live on a permanent basis in 94 countries and territories outside of Vietnam, though other estimates are between 2.7 and 3 million. In January 2008 VCP General Secretary Nong Duc Manh said that Vietnam's recent economic achievements were much assisted by the "patriotic" efforts of returned exiles.[89] According to the Vietnamese Ministry of Foreign Affairs (MFA), some 1.3 million Vietnamese reside in the United States. The VCP and government say they "consider the overseas Vietnamese community (Viet Kiew) an integrated part of and invaluable resource for the Vietnamese national community" and that "many policies and measures are being reviewed and adjusted to create better conditions for overseas Vietnamese, particularly for intellectuals and businesspeople to return and cooperate with domestic partners." An MFA news release in mid-2008 reported that Vietnamese Americans have supported normalization of U.S.–Vietnam ties and that four hundred U.S. overseas Vietnamese businesses have registered with Vietnam's Domestic Investment Encouragement Law with a total of $47 million. Twenty other projects under the Foreign Investment Law have a total capital of US$85 million. In 2007 some 209,826 Vietnamese Americans visited Vietnam, and remittances from Vietnamese in the United States came to $3.85 million, some 70 percent of the total overseas Vietnamese remittances during the year.[90]

But for all this positive news from Hanoi, relations between the VCP-controlled country and the Vietnamese who left three to four decades ago under the most adverse of circumstances have often not been good. When you consider that the estimated incomes of overseas Vietnamese amount to something like $50 billion annually, several hundred million in investments isn't much. To some degree, there is a corresponding hostility and jealousy toward those who left on the part of some who remained in Vietnam. Many overseas Vietnamese also were long put off by harassment for bribes by some officials and by personal affronts. In a sense, the level of hostility toward the conquering VCP is more similar to that toward Castro on the part of Cubans who fled Cuba after 1959 than to the hostility toward the communist regime in Beijing by overseas Chinese, so many of whom had been abroad for many decades. One very practical consequence of this hostility is that, while overseas Chinese immediately became the main investors in post-Mao reforming China, overseas Vietnamese have not done the same in *doi moi* Vietnam. Another reason for this disparity in investment is the fact that overseas Chinese were the only ones who had the connections to invest safely in China immediately after Mao. On the other hand, many *non*-Vietnamese investors in many countries had long been eager to explore and make large investments in the new Vietnam.

One Vietnamese-American businessman has noted that, ironically, the risks for Vietnamese overseas investors are often higher than for other foreign investors and are concentrated mainly in three areas: inadequate legal protection, questionable business opportunities, and iffy competitive advantages. A San Jose, California, Vietnamese American involved in real estate deals in Ho Chi Minh City said, "If you don't have connections, you can't work here."[91]

PART IV

Special Challenges for Small and Medium-Sized Enterprises

AS AN INTRODUCTION to our final examination of some specific problems faced by micro, small, and medium-sized businesses in Vietnam, it is worth noting that one never hears of SMLE surveys. That is because the "L" would stand for *large*, and very few large firms in Vietnam are owned by private Vietnamese individuals or groups. More and more microbusinesses are moving up, so to speak, to become formal small enterprises. Some small enterprises climb up to be medium-sized enterprises. But almost none of the medium-sized enterprises become large. Recognizing the reality of this glass ceiling, and searching for its reasons, helps to put Vietnam's ultimate prospects into perspective. Vast changes have occurred in Vietnam since *doi moi,* many of which I have seen personally on visits since the U.S. embargo was lifted. Yet some government actions, and some public opinion, leave open the question of whether the country's ease of doing business, as measured by the World Bank, will ever get anywhere near that of Vietnam's very close neighbors, Singapore and Hong Kong, with their overwhelmingly ethnic Chinese population.

Let's take another look at how Vietnam ranks in recent international ratings of its business environment. These show slight improvements over the year before: The World Economic Forum's *Global Competitiveness Report 2007–2008* ranks Vietnam 68 among 131 countries; *Doing Business 2008* from the World Bank and the International Finance Corporation puts Vietnam at 91 among 178 nations in the ease of doing business; and the *2008 Index of Economic Freedom* published by the Heritage Foundation rates Vietnam 135 among 157 nations measured.

Looking further at the *Doing Business 2008* report, which goes into greater detail than the other reports, we see that while tiger cub Vietnam has come a long way, it is still far behind the world's or the region's front-runners. The top ten in the ease-of-doing-business sweepstakes are Singapore, New Zealand, United States, Hong Kong, Denmark, United Kingdom, Canada, Ireland, Australia, and Iceland. Vietnam is ranked 91 in this category, and China, with which Vietnam is so often compared, is 83, both improvements over past years. In other categories, among the 175 countries in the comparison, Vietnam was ranked 97 in starting a business, 63 in dealing with licenses, 84 in employing workers, 38 in registering property, 48 in getting credit, 165 in protecting investors, 128 in paying taxes, 63 in trading across borders, 40 on enforcing contracts, and 121 on closing a business. These ratings give a good sense of most of the challenges faced by small and medium-sized enterprises (SMEs) and others in Vietnam today.

For the sake of international context, it is worth noting that in the various categories just listed, the world has no "straight A's"; that is, every one of the top ten countries in the general ease of doing business tally has at least a couple of double-digit rankings. For example, Hong Kong, which is ranked 4 in ease of doing business, is 60 in dealing with licenses, and the United Kingdom, with an overall rating of 6, is 54 in licenses. Japan, which is 12 in overall ease of doing business, is 105 in paying taxes, and Switzerland, which is 16 in overall ease of doing business, is 158 in protecting investors.

13

Access to
the "People's Land"

IN VIETNAM, land ownership is collective, while land use and building rights in Vietnam can be held privately. That is, all land is owned collectively and managed by the state. Land rights have been long in coming in Vietnam, and they are not secure yet. The first important preliminary land legislation was in 1988, the first land law was in 1993, the next land law was passed in 2003 and implemented in 2004, and use rights, spelled out in the Land Law of 2003, deal with transfers, leases, mortgages, inheritance, transformations, and bequests. Since 2007, land leases for foreigners are a maximum of seventy years. One of the key problems for entrepreneurs in Vietnam today, and thus for the country as a whole, is getting land for one's enterprise. The Heritage Foundation's *2008 Index of Economic Freedom* gave Vietnam a score of 10 percent on the protection and facilitation of property rights. The deep roots of this problem are in the state land ownership policies of the Soviet period, as well as in the VCP's continuing support for socialist institutions and objectives on a national level.[92] In 2007 the deputy director of the Land Department of the Ministry of Natural Resources and Environment, Dao Trung Chinh, admitted that "SMEs can rarely find access to land in good locations, nor is there adequate availability of large-sized plots. . . . Land planning and zoning still needs a lot of work." At the same time, Vu Duy Thai, chairman of the Hanoi Trade and Industry Association, said, "Private businesses in need of land usually have to sub-lease unused land from SOEs for a high price and on non-secured terms."[93] Still, as the *Economist* reported in its April 24,

2008, special report on Vietnam, "Private firms are bounding ahead despite bureaucracy, corruption, poor regulation, a feeble legal system and a creaking infrastructure."

At the end of the French colonial period, roughly half of the land in Vietnam was in the hands of the French or their sympathizers. With independence, that land, much of it simply abandoned or donated to the state, was taken over by the new VCP government. What remained in private hands was seized with the implementation of the 1953 Land Reform Law, often accompanied by widespread violence. The popularity of the new communist regime, already high because it had thrown out the French, increased when this land was redistributed to farmers, as had occurred during early land reform in China. But then, during the same years as China's disastrous Great Leap Forward and People's Communes, 1958 to 1960, the land was seized again by the state, the right to private ownership was abolished, and agriculture was collectivized. In North Vietnam some 85 percent of the households had been collectivized by 1960, and 68 percent of the land area was cultivated by more than 40,000 cooperatives. When the South was conquered by the North, collectivization became the policy there as well, though it was not so thoroughly implemented. Predictably, these policies effectively guaranteed low productivity, inefficiency, shortages, and indeed the utter failure that not only plagued a generation of Vietnamese but still haunts the people and government today as other, usually more productive schemes are being attempted. For example, the *Markets & Development Bulletin* of May 2005 ticks off eleven obstacles the poor face in getting formal land titles, ranging from high formal and informal fees to local government intervention to inaccurate plot measurements.

Today, land is still regarded as the property of the people as a whole, with the state acting as their representative owner. The people's right to use their land is granted by the state for periods of decades, depending on the use made of the plot, with the lease renewable so long as the property is still being used in a way approved of by the state. The government grants permanent land use for residential land and several other categories. In practice, a major portion of Vietnam's land is still allocated and controlled according to government decisions made long ago for a system that abjectly failed, taking a heavy toll on individuals and on the growth and potential of the Vietnamese economy. On November 24, 2006, Minister of Natural Resources and Environment Mai Ai Truc, quoted by *VietnamNet Bridge* on November 25, 2006, told the National Assembly that corruption and wastefulness are the most pressing problems in land management and usage today.

In urban areas, inadequate land is designated for commercial and industrial use, in large part because most of it is in the hands of the state-owned enterprises (SOEs). An Investment Climate Survey found that if one considers firms with 250 or more employees, SOEs averaged five times more land than private enterprises.[94] In rural areas, the Land Law of 1988 called for distribution of land to families in the countryside, but the effort to do so equitably led to serious property fragmentation, so that the average rural household in northern Vietnam has 6.5 separate and usually separated plots of land, none large.[95] It was hoped that issuing transferable Land-Use Right Certificates (LURCs), discussed later, would lead to property exchanges that would reduce the problem, but this has not happened. Irrigation complications, government-mandated crop choices, and credit constraints have often stood in the way so that conversion to industrial use is impossible or very slow and often riddled with corruption. There is little industrial land in cities that is not already occupied by SOEs, and efforts to convert agricultural land are slow and complicated. When land does open up, SOEs usually get the first crack at it. The World Bank's *Vietnam Development Report* 2006 concluded that 95 percent of the land under lease to organizations in Hanoi is in the hands of SOEs, with 5 percent left for private enterprises, cooperatives, and other production groups.[96] The new Land Law mandates that the SOEs must return whatever land they are not using to the state, but few do so.

Enter the LURCs, sometimes called Red Books, which have been issued to households since the implementation of the Land Law of 1993.

These LURCs are the official title papers needed for many transactions to be legal or possible at all. For example, they are needed when putting land up as collateral to borrow capital to launch or develop a private enterprise. But the titling is far from complete, particularly in urban areas, and the LURCs themselves are often out of date, inaccurate, or incomplete, as when women's names are left off. Thus, some transactions involving land are virtually impossible, enormously complicated, or take place illegally.[97] A 2004 revision of the Land Law has improved conditions somewhat by making it legal to lease, sublease, transfer, or bequeath a LURC, if you have one, but as indicated earlier this is easier said than done, and it raises the question of what is to be done when the expiration date arrives. A 2007 study by the Ministry of Planning and Investment's Central Institute for Economic Management (CIEM) acknowledged that Red Books still have not been issued for all plots, that there are great differences across regions, and that only 9 percent of the plots surveyed have two names in the book, which means that women have been omitted.[98]

According to a Mekong Private Sector Development Facility study of business registration, a quarter of the 300 firms surveyed indicated that finding the right premises or land was the most difficult problem they faced in starting their business, and that land was the second most serious problem (behind financing) in the composite question of starting and operating a business. The problem is so pervasive that even when it is resolved it often significantly affects the size of the firm (the less land needed, the less trouble) and even the type of business chosen, since services and trade usually require less space to operate. Tellingly, of the firms the MPDF surveyed, only 10 percent were on their own land. Roughly half of the firms were on rented land, and the remainder were on land owned privately by the owner of the enterprise. The property of business owners was usually very small and offered little or no space for expansion. The most common way to acquire land today is through the direct transfer of title to the new owner for an agreed-upon price. In one sample, some 65 percent of SMEs had used this procedure for recent land acquisition.[99]

Rented land, from private landowners or SOEs, is a particular headache and causes ongoing difficulties for most firms. SOEs are the best source of land rentals for manufacturing and trading (for warehouses) firms that need a lot of space. Surveys by the U.S. Agency for International Development, the MPDF, and others show that the maximum rental contracts from SOEs were for ten years, but most were much shorter. Such short terms greatly discouraged both the investment of significant amounts of fixed capital and the expansion of operations. Some of the SOEs rented the land illegally, and so rent for the space could not be claimed as a business expense at tax time, nor could the costs of utilities. And since the rent was unofficial, courts could never be involved in resolving any legal disputes. This is just one of the reasons negotiations are the preferred way to settle legal differences.

Renting from private landowners is usually far worse, however, since contracts are usually for from six months to one year. Good employees leave or altogether shun such businesses, since they are subject to being laid off with little or no notice. Only 15 percent of the enterprises surveyed by the MPDF even tried to buy land from the government. First, very little land is available for business purposes, and when some is available, small businesses cannot afford to buy it, in part because of the great difficulties they usually have in getting credit. Also, the bureaucratic complications of even trying were daunting, and the rules of the game often changed in the course of negotiations.

The government has conducted large-scale conversions of agricultural land for industrial and commercial use. By 2005, land had been taken from some 100,000 households, some of which were pleased and some greatly inconvenienced, for the development of 190 industrial zones and clusters.[100] Many poor households were negatively affected by the conversion process, because they lost their agricultural occupations and had to seek other work in other places. The justification for the process, as stated in the *Markets & Development Bulletin*: "Improving access to land is a vital requirement for private sector development, economic growth, job creation and poverty reduction." But "an important policy issue arises of how to mediate the interests and rights of farming households and those of private enterprises and their employees. The state has a crucial role in balancing these interests in an efficient, transparent and consistent manner." [101]

14

Funding and Credit, If You Can Get It

MONEY IS A PROBLEM for businesses all over the world, but in Vietnam there are a lot of wrinkles that the typical American cannot even imagine. A survey conducted by the Central Institute for Economic Management (CIEM) and Denmark's Danida organization revealed that access to bank loans is the most difficult problem faced by SMEs. Many of the latter said that what they most want from state authorities is support in accessing bank credit. Other enterprises sought irregular capital, and some of them also had difficulties in borrowing money. Many enterprises said that they never sought capital from banks, because they did not have suitable mortgaged assets, they considered procedures too complicated, or they found the interest rates too high. The poll showed that 69% of bank loans they did receive came from state-owned banks. SMEs had a high percentage of "underground expenses," that is, 41% said that they have paid bribes to state officials, though they considered the costs small when compared to total revenue.[102]

Since the private businesses began, the obstacles have been nearly overwhelming, particularly for people who had no experience with founding and running a business, which at first was everyone. The majority of the companies interviewed by the MPDF were long unable to borrow from banks, though that seems slowly to be changing for the better. Thus, would-be entrepreneurs had to save and/or borrow from family, friends, or loan sharks. Predictably, they have had to start businesses that do not require substantial capital, on minimal land with little or no hope of expanding beyond small or medium size, though in fact many businesspeople don't really have the entrepreneurial spirit, for better or worse, and seem satisfied with just enough business to support their families.

In contrast, a Danish Development Assistance study released in late 2007 showed that credit to SMEs has increased in recent years and that fewer firms were denied credit than in 2002. The "problem" is the rapid growth of the private sector, which has increased the demand for credit. Thus, although the percentage of denials is unchanged and about one-fourth of SMEs are "credit restrained," the underlying numbers are larger because there are more businesses. What this means is that the formal financial sector is just managing to keep up with growth, which is not good enough, since SMEs underpin the growth process of Vietnam.[103]

Collateral is a major barrier: The majority of SMEs lack the security required for a loan, and the application process has been very complicated and time-consuming. Some entrepreneurs in the survey were willing to put up their homes or other property as collateral, though this can become very complicated if one lacks the proper title deeds, as many do, and has to prove one's ownership of the property. Even when a loan was granted, it was often for only a small fraction of the home's real value. Some SMEs had to borrow from banks through a third party, usually an SOE, in exchange for a commission and the interest payment on the loan. A CIEM study released in late 2007 noted that household savings, mostly held in cash in homes, are not available for investment purposes and called for teaching people how to make their cash holdings productive for investment purposes.[104]

Then there is taxation, which the World Bank's *Vietnam Development Report 2008* (VDR 2008) says is "an area currently undergoing a dramatic overhaul." Of course, businesses almost everywhere have to pay taxes, but in Vietnam the challenges are far more numerous and more serious than most Americans, for all our frustrations with our own IRS, can imagine. The VDR 2008 indicated that the burden of taxes "appears to be higher for domestic private enterprises, for small firms and for those located in rural areas. . . . Whether this pattern is due to deliberate incentives, to weak tax administration or to evasion is unclear. But whatever the reasons, imposing a higher (actual) tax burden on small firms, private businesses or enterprises located in rural areas does not seem to be in the best interest of Vietnam." Finally, the VDR 2008 reported that "Vietnam has adopted an ambitious agenda to modernize tax administration, but implementation will be challenging," to say the least.[105]

The MPDF reports that for many private firms the tax process seems to be an elaborate game of bargaining between the company and the tax officials, with the latter holding all the high cards. Taxes must be paid in advance at the beginning of the year, and since the tax officials don't trust the business owners, they simply impose whatever tax they think is reasonable. According to reports, the amount is invariably higher than the year before, quite irrespective of whether the business has prospered or declined in the interim. In addition to the problem of the red invoice books discussed later, SME owners and accountants often find tax officials very problematic, as will be illustrated in the later walk-through of a business registration.

Also, the entrepreneur must purchase value-added tax (VAT) red invoice books if he wishes to sell his product to SOEs, government organizations, and some other potential clients, as well as to document funds going in and out for tax and other purposes. Informal businesses can't buy red invoices at all, while formal SMEs often find the process of buying them a terrible bureaucratic hassle, both burdensome and expensive. Often a firm is permitted to buy only one book (50 to 100 invoices) at a time, thus necessitating repeated visits to the agency to buy new ones, the frequency depending, of course, on the firm's level of activity. The managing director him- or herself sometimes has to show up and laboriously prove his or her legitimacy. An MPDF survey found that buying a single book might require several visits to the agency.[106]

15

Walking Through a Business Registration

THE VIETNAMESE GOVERNMENT'S Ministry of Planning and Investment, through its Agency for SME Development, walks the potential businessperson through the process of opening and running a business. A great deal of information is provided in this walk-through, ranging from an introduction to critical legislation to the business options available under the 2005–6 enterprise legislation to possible legal consultants, though not all of the potential hitches are elaborated.[107] This section covers much of the same ground, but it describes the process as experienced by the individuals interviewed by MPDF analysts. Building on the earlier comments about the state of the law, banking, registrations, land, funding, and other matters, this description of the process required for formalizing an SME will give a more personal feel for what it is like to try to start a business in Vietnam—that is, to be a practicing entrepreneur. This description, of course, involves just what it takes to get started in a formal business, not continuing to operate after registration is finally completed.

The MPDF leads the way in its previously cited study, *Behind the Headline Numbers: Business Registration and Startup in Vietnam,* published in mid-2005. There are four steps to this process: (1) register for a business certificate from the local Department of Planning and Investment, this action then turning up in the next National Business Information Center (NBIC) report; (2) get a corporate seal made and register it at the local police station; (3) receive a company tax code from the local tax office; and (4) purchase a red invoice book from the tax office.

This doesn't sound like a big deal, but in one survey the MPDF found that on average it took a firm about fifty days to complete the registration and start-up process. According to *Doing Business 2007,* starting a business in Canada takes one day, in Australia it takes two, and in the United States and New Zealand it takes three. There are many reasons for the length of the process in Vietnam, but two of them are that each step must be taken in a different place, and most must be done in sequence; in other words, each step must be completed before the next one can begin. One option is to hire a service provider, and there are increasing numbers of these, of varying quality, particularly in the big cities. In 2005 the provider (such as a law firm) typically charged about US$140 to handle the entire process, which for the provider with experience and connections averaged twenty-three days instead of fifty. Our walk-through will be without the aid of a provider and is based on the experiences of twenty-five emerging enterprises examined by the MPDF.

(1) **Registering.** On average, it took businesses fourteen to twenty days to accomplish this first step. The office was very busy, and the half or so who paid a relatively small unofficial fee, which some might call a bribe, got through more quickly than those who did not. One applicant who would not pay, though he was openly encouraged to do so by officials in the office, needed two months to complete this stage. Paying the fee also got closer cooperation from the officials in filling out registration documents, and here the problem was similar to the one in the tax office. If you paid your dues under the table, all problems were straightened out at once, instead of one problem each time you came in if you paid no unofficial fee.

(2) **Registering a company seal.** Only after finishing step 1 could the applicant go to the local Department of Police to register the official company seal. Some paid an unofficial fee to the police, some did not, but no one had any particular problem getting through. Still, the average time to do this was ten days.

(3) **Obtaining a tax code.** It usually took fifteen days to register for a tax code at the local Department of Taxation. This code is used for both

the VAT and corporate income tax. The majority of firms interviewed said they had no particular problem here, though some had to go back several times and pay an unofficial fee. One woman applying said, "At first, they asked us to come back over and over again. But then we gave them something under the table, not much, and it was done. You know, it is an unwritten law. . . . We see these procedures as simply something that must be done, we do not think of them as a problem."

(4) **Purchasing the red invoice book.** This was usually a complicated and frustrating step. At the purchase of the first red invoice book, which was discussed earlier, the company director had to be present to prove he was who he said he was. About half the applicants paid an unofficial fee.

A second MPDF registration test-run, this time in Bac Ninh province, took 126 detailed steps over a 32-day period, somewhat shorter than the MPDF's experience just described and shorter than the time reported in the World Bank's *Doing Business 2005* for registering in Hanoi. In the end, the MPDF estimates that in Vietnam it generally takes thirty-five to fifty days to register, at a high expense to the registering party.

In its *Bulletin* of August 2006, the MPDF argued the importance of registering a business as follows. First, formal enterprises have less to hide from government inspectors and thus can afford to grow larger, which enhances their impact. According to *Doing Business 2005*, cited in the *Bulletin*, informal enterprises typically produce 40 percent less than businesses in the formal economy. Second, registered businesses have easier access to bank credit and to useful public services, and can export directly. Third, registered businesses pay taxes that increase the government tax base and allow the state to lower the tax burden on all firms.

If it is possible to register a new business in just a couple of days in Canada and Australia, why can't the same be done in Vietnam? The problems range from the history and continuation of bureaucratic red tape and corruption, particularly dating to the early communist period, to the still uneven support for the business process itself by many laws, individuals in power, and institutions around the country. Also, the extra time is necessary because the different branches of the government do not communicate with each other. As a result, prospective businesspeople have to carry out the registration process in sequence, only one of the problems being that they often have to fill out forms with the same information in several or all of the offices they visit. They also have to do it all in person, which means they must spend many days going to the same agencies multiple times instead of planning or working. It would be far better to have a one-stop shop where all procedures could be accomplished in one place both quickly and efficiently.

Indeed, the MPDF demonstrated the value of the one-stop procedure so convincingly with its pilot project in Bac Ninh province, where the process still took thirty-two days, that the Ministry of Planning and Investment commissioned the organization to provide technical assistance to a government task force responsible for streamlining registration around the country.[108] This is far from the first time Vietnamese officials have bought into a program developed by an international advisory group.

A survey in late 2007 showed that 35 to 45 percent of SMEs need to borrow capital but up to 19 percent have met difficulties with or been rejected when they approached banks. The main reason given by banks is they are afraid of high risks, inefficiency, and lack of transparency, as if the SOEs weren't as bad or worse. Still, much has been made since mid-2007 of greater SME access to business funding. The general director of Incombank said in December 2007 that commercial banks are focusing more on SMEs as an increasingly important engine of growth. He said SMEs made up 60 percent of Incombank's commercial customers and 50 percent of its outstanding loans. In early 2008 the International Finance Corporation, which has been one of the strongest supporters of SMEs, announced that it had given a loan of about US$20 million to the Technological and Commercial Joint Stock Bank (Techcombank) to support SMEs.

16

Vietnamese Surprises

VIETNAMESE ATTITUDES toward the registration pro-
cess are sometimes a surprise to international advisers and organizations
and indeed are different from the attitudes found in many neighboring
countries. Take business licensing, for example, which has been much
criticized by foreign advisers for the number of licenses needed and the
time it takes to get them. In the Enterprise Law of 2000, the government
itself sought to cut back the number of licenses required by a businessperson, and the number was reduced briefly until various levels of government began adding new licenses and sublicenses. The MPDF itself
once wrote that Vietnam urgently needs a legal framework to govern
the issuance and implementation of business licensing. After many had
devoted considerable attention to, for example, the need to streamline
business licensing, a major Investment Climate Survey (ICS) found
that many Vietnamese take licensing and other such matters quite in
stride. In fact the ICS showed that Vietnamese were not nearly as wor-
ried about licensing, permits, corruption, and the legal system as many
of their international advisers said they should be.[109]

Perhaps the Vietnamese lack of intense concern about these matters is not all that surprising, though whether it is good for the long-
term prospects of the nation's development may be a different matter.
Acceptance of this kind of government involvement in one's daily life,
including one's business, is completely within the national tradition,
not least the basic outlook deriving from Imperial Confucianism. It
can also be traced to the VCP and to people's long-term acceptance of

the need to keep out of the way while the government does whatever it wishes. Then, too, it can be traced to good manners and a degree of common sense. Why shouldn't the officials in the tax office or police station get a small tip for helping out if we tip a taxi driver or waitress who has simply been doing his or her job? And finally, it may be due to the fact that the Vietnamese have not been in the reform process as long as most of their East and Southeast Asian neighbors. They may become increasingly fed up with delays as time passes.

PART V

Confronting the World

17

Vietnam–U.S. Relations

FOR TWENTY YEARS after the end of the Vietnam War
in 1975, the United States had no formal relations with Vietnam. In February 1994, President Bill Clinton lifted the trade embargo, responding
to increasing Vietnamese cooperation in searching for American prison-
ers of war and those missing in action, although more than 1,300 remain
unaccounted for. Clinton formally normalized diplomatic relations in
July 1995. In March 1998 he granted the Jackson-Vanik waiver to Vietnam, giving Vietnam normal trading rights, but on a basis that must
be renewed annually. In October 2000, Clinton became the first U.S.
president to visit Vietnam since the end of the war. In December 2001 a
U.S.–Vietnam Bilateral Trade Agreement took force, an action that led
to rapidly expanding bilateral trade and U.S. investment. Assistant Secretary of State Christopher Hill told the U.S. Senate Committee on Foreign Relations in March 2008 that the United States has "encouraged
this new orientation and has been actively facilitating change in Vietnam for over a decade through our development assistance and trade
policy," though Washington has remained critical of many of Vietnam's
civil and human rights actions.[110]

Vietnam's Prime Minister Phan Van Khai visited George W. Bush in
the White House in June 2005, and President Nguyen Minh Triet came
to the United States in June 2007. In November 2006, the United States
removed Vietnam from the list of countries that severely repress religion
and Hanoi hosted the Asia-Pacific Economic Cooperation (APEC). In

January 2007, the U.S. Congress approved permanent normal trade relations (PNTR) for Vietnam, meaning that the country now has full trading rights without the previously required annual reviews by Congress, and in June 2007 the two countries concluded a Trade and Investment Framework Agreement (TIFA) to support implementation of previous agreements and identify new opportunities for trade and investment. U.S. investments in Vietnam, some via third countries, were about $4 billion in 2006 and are expected to reach $8 billion in 2008. The United States now ranks ninth among the seventy-five countries and territories that have invested in Vietnam. Vietnam's accession to the World Trade Organization and the PNTR have helped push two-way trade up to $12.5 billion in 2007, an increase of 29 percent over 2006. American naval ships have been visiting Vietnamese ports since 2003, and several cooperative agreements dealing with terrorism and other issues have been reached between the militaries of the two countries. And Vietnam is an increasingly popular U.S.—and world—tourist destination.

18

Joining the World Trade Organization

VIETNAM FIRST APPLIED for membership in the WTO in 1995. Its application was finally fully accepted at the end of October 2006, and official membership came in mid-January 2007. This membership was the obvious and necessary next step for a country that lives so much on trade and is ever more involved in the international market system. Joining has given Vietnam equal access to world markets, not least in the United States, and has already thrown wide the door to increasing foreign investment.

A month before Vietnam's entry into the WTO, participants in a Vietnam Business Forum in Hanoi noted quite accurately some of the country's main strengths and weaknesses. Among the former are the country's strategic location, political stability, quite good macroeconomic management, inexpensive labor force, and market growth potential, as well as its being an alternative to China. Its remaining problems include regional competitiveness, poor infrastructure, an inadequately educated labor force, weak intellectual property protection, substantial corruption, and an opaque legal system. A recurring complaint for years has been the disparity between laws on the books and how they are irregularly enforced.[111] After the final entry negotiations had been completed, Vietnamese Vice Trade Minister Tran Duc Minh remarked that the most important things for Vietnam to do were to improve management capability, economic efficiency, and competitiveness.[112]

After eighteen months of WTO membership, it is clear that many positive changes have occurred, at least in part because of WTO membership, and some problems have also emerged. The Swiss banking corporation Credit Suisse said Vietnamese structural reform, political stability, pricing advantages, low costs, and a young population had brought one of the largest gross domestic product (GDP) expansions in the world, with a growth rate over the past decade of 7.1 percent annually. All of these factors made Vietnam an extremely attractive country for investors, particularly after its entry into the WTO. The March 2008 Leap Forward Vietnam Business Leadership Forum concluded that Vietnam ranked sixth in the world in attracting foreign direct investment (FDI). In the final 11 months of 2007, Vietnam attracted FDI valued at US $15 billion. Among the 1,283 newly licensed projects during this period in 51 cities and provinces, 55 relatively large ones accounted for $9.6 billion. According to a Vietnam Foreign Ministry report, the *World Investment Report 2007*, published by the United Nations Convention on Trade and Development (UNCTAD), 11% of transnational corporations say Vietnam is their favored FDI destination in upcoming years. The UN report continues that Vietnam ranks 6 among 141 economies surveyed as an attractive investment location, following China, India, the US, Russia, and Brazil. The attraction, according to the Foreign Ministry, is not only in the manufacturing sector, though that is the leading sector, but also in the service, banking, and finance sectors.[113]

The most obvious negative development was the rapid rise in inflation, and what that may mean about the nation's monetary and exchange rate policy. Some blame the inflation more on the influx of so much money, soaring world prices for petroleum, and other factors than on gross delinquency on the part of Vietnam's macroeconomic team. Other negative factors were a 2.5-fold increase in the trade deficit, to $12.4 billion, and all the problems mentioned in this study, from legal to educational to administrative and the challenges of competitiveness.

PART VI

Conclusions and Observations

WHAT CONCLUSIONS, some more tentative than others, can we draw from the recent Vietnamese experience with market reforms and entrepreneurship?

• The essential time frame for understanding Vietnam's present and its prospects for the future does not begin twenty or so years ago with renovation or reforms, but fifty years ago when the communists took over or, indeed, more than two thousand years back when China ruled the territory of what is now Vietnam. That Chinese connection resulted in Vietnam's even now having a culture and institutions that have been held back by and driven ahead by Confucian tradition as adapted over time to suit Vietnam's own civilization.[110]

• The two factors most affecting the prospects for market-oriented reform and the successful emergence of private enterprise in Vietnam are (1) the globalization of the current period and the outreach of the world into the cities and countryside of Vietnam and (2) the Vietnamese reaction to that phenomenon. That reaction is complex, for it is at once welcoming, cautious, and hostile. On the one hand, it offers the reality of economic progress and access to the necessities of life, and hope for very much more. One particularly impressive accomplishment in Vietnam has been one of the most successful antipoverty campaigns ever undertaken anywhere, raising about two-thirds of those who lived in poverty two decades ago into the land of the living by combating both the antiproductive aspects of tradition and the needless poverty still imposed to some degree by the dead economic hand of Ho Chi Minh and his followers.

On the other hand, Vietnam's encounter with the world also represents a challenge to the more group-oriented values deriving originally from Confucianism, with the result often being a confrontation between competitive global forces and these values. The small and medium-sized private enterprises are often on the cutting edge of this encounter, introducing a heightened role for individuals, families, and private business organizations that can create jobs and prosperity for the people in general. The government has facilitated SME activities in some respects, but also retains some age-old, state-centered paternalistic perspectives and institutions, ranging from a distrust of individual initiative to rampant corruption and absence of transparency. The overall vision essential to fully successful reform is often overpowered by thought and self-serving actions that undercut otherwise potentially productive programs and change.

• Just as Vietnam's rapid emergence was dependent on post–Cold War globalization, so to an as yet undetermined degree is it dependent on the continuation of international contacts generally and commercial relations specifically. An international crisis deriving from a serious downturn in the U.S. economy, for example, or a major conflict in Asia, as between any combination of China, the United States, Taiwan, and/or North Korea, not to mention countries in Southeast Asia itself, could suddenly throw everyone back into an earlier and less hopeful era.

• Productive reforms must, of course, reflect best practice in fields as various as macroeconomic policy and high technology, and must provide a welcome setting for foreign investment and domestic private enterprise. But in the end a critical lesson of modern Vietnam is that ideas and political will themselves have profound consequences. The ideas of the first three decades of Vietnam Communist Party (VCP) rule, for example, were in large part those of the Soviet theorists and party hacks who created the Soviet bloc's dead-handed economics and state-craft around the world. These ideas and institutions were hopelessly out of touch with reality from the beginning, despite their juvenile claims to being scientific, and they prompted policies that led to tragic economic, social, and other outcomes. One cannot discount the wars of the period and the terrible destruction they caused, but Soviet-inspired VCP policies made things far worse than they need have been, and they would have done so even if the wars had never occurred. Had there been no wars in Vietnam and the rest of the region, it probably just would have taken longer for the country's economy to collapse and be reformed. The thrust of VCP ideas during the past two decades, in contrast, has been much more realistic and has led to policies that have greatly improved standards of living and prospects for the country. Will it remain progressive into the future, and indeed become more so, and how might things change during a domestic or international crisis?

• Most international observers agreed until recently that despite some bouts with rather high single-digit inflation, the country could be counted on to demonstrate macroeconomic stability. This belief promoted much progress in some services, including electricity and telecommunications, and low crime rates, which in turn brought significantly better lives to people and began laying a foundation for future reforms and prosperity. But the inflation rate of recent years has thrust a threatening reality onto the nation that must be confronted openly and realistically, beginning yesterday. Studies by Harvard University and the Economist Intelligence Unit (EIU) correctly conclude that unless economic decisions are both well informed and separated from political power and interests, and development efforts and funds are used effectively, constructive reform will be seriously impeded and the country will begin to fall back on the development front. The EIU sees annual growth declining to 5.1 percent annually for the 2011–2020 period.[114]

• Although much has gone well in the past twenty years, the negatives are also clear, and efforts to recover from some of the mistakes of the past are often slow in paying off, when they do so at all. The greatest obstacles to quicker and more effective reform today, and to better ratings in the international scorecards, are some enduring ideas and the domestic economic legacies of Uncle Ho and Le Duan, all linked to certain unproductive aspects of traditional beliefs and the resulting institutions. More specifically, these are the disastrous collectivization of agriculture, now largely reversed but with enduring negative consequences; the doling out of so much land to state-owned enterprises (SOEs) under inefficient state control, which continues in important respects despite reforms; and the creation of banks whose primary purpose for many years was to feed pep pills to moribund SOE dinosaurs. So far these dinosaurs, even dressed up today as equitized enterprises, remain in many ways more liabilities than assets with respect to national development. They still squeeze funds from the nation to sustain their inefficient and often shoddy production, even as they impede the private enterprises, very importantly through trade favoritism in 2008, that offer better prospects for eventual broader prosperity. And yet, with the VCP's continuing professions of seeking socialism, with the SOEs as an important factor, and with the banks' involvement in achieving the socialist objectives of the nation, basic questions for the future remain unanswered. Western critiques of SOEs and banks with non-paying loans will seem substantially less compelling, and Washington's arrogance with respect the organization and management of a national economy will be less welcome, though some of the recommendations will still be correct, in the wake of the collapse of the U.S. financial system in late-2008

• Major government efforts have been made to create an atmosphere conducive to entrepreneurship and private-sector development. As shown in this report, much progress has been made, not least because so many of the Vietnamese people have risen to the challenge of starting businesses to improve their personal and family lives and thus advance the productivity of the nation. But inertia, the government's continuing dedication to making Vietnam in some form "socialist," which has its appeals in traditional thinking, makes the prospects for the long-term success of private enterprise uncertain. The lack of accurate statistics on what is actually happening in the development of household enterprises and small and medium-sized enterprises (SMEs) complicates problems of reform, in some respects giving a more positive coloration to developments than is warranted. These impediments to entrepreneurship must be confronted if the country is to experience maximum possible development, and there are signs, such as the attention paid to the Vietnam Competitiveness Initiative and other non-governmental projects, that progress is being made. Will the people and government really want to press for maximum growth, however, or will they resist for cultural, power, and selfish reasons? Or will the people and government find a way to square this circle, as the Chinese, in their way, are trying to do?

• Vietnam is facing a strong challenge with its recent admission to the World Trade Organization. The advantages for Vietnam of the new markets that have opened up have been considerable, and the foreign technology investments it has been able to attract suggest that Vietnam is competing better with some of its neighbors than might have been expected. But will this trend continue and expand? The government is still preventing the most industrious entrepreneurs from going as far as they are capable of going, and if those people go under, leaving mainly the SOEs and foreign enterprises, the latter will be the only ones that can compete internationally. The bright prospect being realized in part is that WTO and other pressures will get the Hanoi government to act more quickly and forcefully to weed out the inefficient and promote the industrious, to enact and enforce legal and institutional changes that will keep Vietnam developing, and yet to find ways to avoid destroying an environment that is already showing serious signs of strain in the cities and countryside. One of the most serious failures of the VCP government has been its refusal to undertake quality education reform. Though education is more widely available than before in Vietnam, its quality at all levels ranges from just adequate to intolerable. Harvard and other foreign institutions have tried to raise the level of academic discourse with very limited success. In August 2008 Japan and the Asian Development Bank announced a plan to develop model research universities in Danang and Hanoi, with Vietnamese government support. We'll see.

• Finally, there are the prospects of squaring the circle, of finding a possible alternative path to development. So far, at least, reforming Asian countries have broken many of the development rules associated with the West. The main common denominators between Western and most successful Asian development experiences have been a recognition of the need for macroeconomic stability and market-oriented policies encouraging international trade and investment. Milton Friedman long argued that progress is dependent on government activity being limited primarily to establishing the framework within which individuals are free to pursue their own objectives. In Asia, however, the government has always played a much more active role, not only traditionally but even in the reforms of recent decades. Even Hong Kong, often Friedman's example of the freest market in the world, had one of the world's highest levels of government-subsidized housing. Since the Emergency Economic Stabilization Act of 2008, by whatever name, the United States has lurched in the direction of Asian government involvement in the national economy.

So Asian governments have usually played a strong role in the reforms of recent decades. In some countries, power has tended to pass from the dominant leader to more popular forums, but comments by today's leaders in Vietnam, as in China, suggest that the government will continue to play an active role in the future, in line with traditional group-oriented thinking and statecraft. Vietnamese leaders continue to say, for example, that SOEs will remain the linchpin of the economy in the future. Will Vietnam, China, and other countries with a very long Confucian tradition be able to find a way to combine an orientation toward paternalism and communitarianism, and a tolerance of significant levels of corruption and inefficiency, with the equally established dedication to education, diligence, and frugality? Will that compromise be found or prove increasingly elusive as economies and global interrelationships expand? Whatever the level of government involvement in Vietnam's future, it is hard to believe that prosperity will be possible without the government's providing a framework for individuals to pursue their own objectives, with the beneficial spillover this will bring to the country as a whole. In the end, Vietnamese leaders must clarify their goals, objectively evaluate what programs best move the people and country toward those goals and then have the will the follow through with the implementation of those programs that work.

Appendix:
A Note on International
Involvement in Vietnam's Reforms

VIETNAM TODAY is awash in foreigners promoting vary-ing types and degrees of reform, innovation, entrepreneurship, and individual private initiative and enterprise. This involvement must be emphasized from the beginning because the very act of involvement has had assorted consequences at all levels throughout the country. With the authorization of the Vietnam Communist Party (VCP) and the gov-ernment, these groups range from many foreign governments, includ-ing the United States, to international organizations like the World Bank, the Asian Development Bank, and the Grameen Bank, to non-governmental organizations (NGOs), innumerable private consultants, and individual researchers like myself involved in American think tanks. Also, many overseas Vietnamese have returned to Vietnam to share their experiences abroad, and their wealth acquired abroad, with people in their original homeland.

On balance, this involvement has been a very positive thing. Most obviously, the international support for reforms has (1) brought new ideas, practices, and other forms of support flooding into the country, at times seeming to overwhelm the eager recipients; (2) by and large led to reforms that have enabled many of the nation's people to become much more productive; (3) to varying degrees contributed toward the improved livelihoods of a major percentage of the population, raising tens of millions out of extreme poverty; and (4) laid the foundation for continuing modernization and growth in the future.

Typically, the outside groups have focused on policy in one or more of the following usually overlapping areas of concern, always necessarily taking into consideration the limits to which the communist government, with its continuing socialist objectives, and the people within their national traditions are willing and able to go. First is education and the transfer of knowledge and conceptions of modernization generally and private enterprise specifically. Second is the advancement of developmental goals by creating the various aspects of a receptive environment for entrepreneurship. Third is institutional reform, seeking to adapt the current administration to the needs of a more market-oriented international system. Fourth is the often difficult delivery of services of all sorts to the people over varying levels of resistance deriving from ignorance, vested interests, inertia, and physical means of communication. Fifth is the harmonization of Vietnam's domestic reforms with the international community, ranging from individual neighboring countries to the United States and such global groupings as the WTO. Finally, the scope of reforms is so vast that neither this nor most other reports on Vietnam today can be close to comprehensive.

International communication with the government and people has ranged from working with individual entrepreneurs to meeting with the top VCP leaders and has involved, among other things, developing a database on what the conditions are and what changes are coming about. In addition to financial support for changes, much of the most important foreign involvement has been in organizing and participating in seminars, panel discussions, and other meetings with Vietnamese ranging from officials to individual businesspeople. The sessions are devoted to entrepreneurship and reform in general, as well as to drawing up new laws and educating individuals and leaders as to how markets can be made to serve individuals and the nation.

At the same time, the process of training and reforming has often been confusing and has fallen short of what foreigners have urged and many Vietnamese entrepreneurs have wanted. In part this has been a result of the enormity of the various challenges faced. (Someone told a World Bank analyst that reform is like repairing a car with the engine running; there is no time to strategize.) The chances of confusion are heightened by the fact that so many of the ideas and institutions were previously unknown to or misunderstood by many Vietnamese recipients, from bureaucrats to potential entrepreneurs. Add to that the fact that the foreign inundation has included some ideas and suggestions that were at odds with each other. The Vietnamese recipients have not always been able to see that two programs offered by different international sources (or even the same source) are incompatible and will cancel each other out and/or create new problems that then will need to be resolved. Finally, some international programs have become self-perpetuating and are a lot "busier" than they are helpful in working out Vietnam's challenges.

Notes

Introduction

1. I consider most of the changes to be best described as reforms and will often use that term in this paper.
2. See Alvaro Vargas Llosa, *Liberty for Latin America*. Nobel economist Douglass North discusses this durability in his *Institutions, Institutional Change, and Economic Performance*. Lawrence Harrison has argued the durability and continuing impact of culture in a series of books beginning with *Underdevelopment Is a State of Mind*. Also see Harrison's article "Hearts, Minds, and Schools."

Survey of Conditions in Vietnam to Mid-2008

3. The economic data in this discussion are drawn largely from reports published by the Asian Development Bank, including *Viet Nam* and Vo Tri Thanh and Pham Chi Quang's *Managing Capital Flows: The Case of Viet Nam*. Other sources were the *Economist's* special report on Vietnam and the Vietnam Development Forum's *Vietnam as an Emerging Industrial Country.*
4. Associated Press, "Foreign Direct Investment in Vietnam." Also see the Ministry of Foreign Affairs, "Outstanding Features of Foreign Direct Investments in Vietnam." Since the British Virgin Islands is one of several offshore financial centers in the Caribbean, it is quite possible that the investment from there reflects "round tripping," that is, the return of Vietnamese capital that has gone abroad to escape foreign exchange controls at home.
5. Ministry of Foreign Affairs, "Vietnam's Overseas Investment."
6. According to the World Bank's *Vietnam Development Report 2008,* the poverty line is defined as "the cost of a food and non-food consumption basket allowing a healthy life."
7. World Bank, *Vietnam Development Report 2008,* Chapter 4.
8. Vietnam Development Forum, *Vietnam as an Emerging Industrial Country.*

Part I

Chapter 1

9. Pham Duy Nghia, "Confucianism and the Conception of the Law in Vietnam," p. 83. Accessed on July 14, 2008 at: *http://www.vdf.org.vn/vdfreport.htm*

10. Vietnamese names can be confusing to foreigners. The name that comes first (e.g., **Ho** Chi Minh) is the surname, usually derived from a Chinese original, though in almost all cases people are referred to by their given name, which comes last. Thus, Professor Pham Duy Nghia in the footnoted sentence is identified as Nghia, VCP General Secretary Nong Duc Manh is called Manh, and, harking back to the days of the Vietnam War, the South Vietnam leader Ngo Dinh Diem was Diem.

11. Pham Duy Nghia, "Confucianism," pp. 79, 77.

12. Fairbank, *China: A New History*, pp. 62–63.

13. Pham Duy Nghia, "Confucianism," p. 83.

14. Pham Duy Nghia, "Confucianism," p. 67. Nghia also discusses characteristics of traditional Vietnamese culture that are similar to those of Confucianism on pp. 80–81.

15. Ratliff, "Confucianism + Capitalism = Economic Development."

16. Some of these points are raised in Harrison, *The Central Liberal Truth*, p. 128.

Chapter 2

17. For example, see Lamb, *Vietnam, Now;* and the autobiography of Trinh Do, *Saigon to San Diego.*

18. Nguyen Khac Vien, *Vietnam: A Long History*, pp. 294, 390–91.

Chapter 3

19. See Abuza, "The Politics of Reform in Vietnam"; and Vo Tri Thanh and Pham Chi Quang, *Managing Capital Flows*, p. 3.

20. 13th APEC Finance Ministerial Meeting opens in Ha Noi. Vietnam Ministry of Foreign Affairs. Accessed on July 14, 2008 at: *http://www.mofa.gov.vn/en/nr040807104143/nr040807105001/ns060908162838?b_start:int=15*

21. Gates says tech can help make Vietnam a miracle economy. AFP, April 2006. Accessed on July 14, 2009 at: *http://findarticles.com/p/articles/mi_kmafp/is_200604/ai_n16241135*

22. PM urges trade sector to develop sustainable export. FDI Vietnam. Accessed on July 14, 2008 at: *http://www.fdivietnam.com.vn/?code=news&id=577&page=news*

23. Abuza, "Vietnam Today."

24. Associated Press, "Silicon Valley Engineer Fights for Freedom."

25. "Vietnam Tightens Grip on Internet," *San Jose Mercury News.*

Chapter 4

26. Constitution of the Socialist Republic of Vietnam: 1992. Shaun Kingsley Malarney notes the VCP draws on Confucian principles to argue leaders are a moral model for the people. A popular party slogan is, "Party members go first, the nation follows (*Dang vien di truoc, lang nuoc di sau*)." See *Culture, Ritual and Revolution in Vietnam.* (New York: RoutledgeCurzon, 2002) p. 64.
27. Nguyen Khac Vien, *Vietnam: A Long History,* pp. 390–91.
28. Hoang Chi Bao, *Socialist Democracy—Goal and Motivation of Renovation.* A friend in the Chinese Academy of Social Sciences recently mentioned a debate in the Communist Party School in Beijing about proper terminology, "Socialism with Chinese Characteristics," which is used today, or "Capitalism with Chinese Characteristics." I suggested they just call it "Development with Chinese Characteristics," and he soon informed me that some thought that a pretty good idea. But it won't happen any time soon, in Beijing or Hanoi.
29. "Objectives of International Economic Integration," *Communist Party of Vietnam Online Newspaper.*

Part II

30. For a discussion of international involvement in Vietnam's reforms, see the Appendix.

Chapter 5

31. Gillespie and Nicholson, *Asian Socialism & Legal Change.* Page numbers cited in the text in this section are from this book. On the broader subject, see Buscaglia and Ratliff, *Law and Economics in Developing Countries.*
32. Nhan Dan, "Vietnam Speeds Up Global Integration with Three More Laws."
33. Tenev et al., *Informality and the Playing Field in Vietnam's Business Sector.*
34. Pham Duy Nghia, "Confucianism," p. 88.

Chapter 6

35. World Bank, *Education in Vietnam,* p. 38.
36. The Harvard Vietnam Program study, *Choosing Success: The Lessons of East and Southeast Asia and Vietnam's Future,* p. 22, with multiple contributors, concludes that Vietnam spends more on education than most countries in the region. Study accessed on Sept. 28, 2008, at: http://www.innovations.harvard.edu/showdoc.html?id=98251 I am grateful to Ann Doyle, senior program officer, and Ben Wilkinson, associate director, of the Harvard University Kennedy School of Government's Vietnam Fulbright Economics Teaching Program (FETP), for sending me comments and materials on the Program's experiences in Vietnam, including a copy of *Choosing Success.* The study is intended as a policy framework for Vietnam's Socioeconomic Development from 2011 to 2020. I also thank Jonathan Pincus, Dean of the FETP, who orchestrated my visit to the program in Ho Chi Minh City in October 2008

37. World Bank. Education in East Asia and Pacific: Vietnam. Accessed on July 14, 2008 at: *http://web.worldbank.org/wbsite/external/countries/eastasiapacificext/exteapregtopedu cation/,,contentMDK:21016301-menuPK:3867184-pagePK:34004173-piPK:34003707-the SitePK:444289,00.html*

38. Asian Development Bank, *Socialist Republic of Viet Nam: Strategic Secondary Education Planning and Cooperation*, p. 134.

39. Vietnam Development Forum. *Vietnam as an Emerging Industrial Country: Policy Scope Toward 2020*, chapter 3. Accessed on July 14, 2008 at: *http://www.vdf.org.vn/vdf report.htm*

40. "Ambitious Generation Steps Forward," *Saigon Times Weekly.*

41. Donald Holsinger, U.S. adviser to the Vietnam Ministry of Education, quoted in VietnamNet Bridge, "Expert Discusses Problems of Vietnam's Education."

42. Vietnamese education fails to satisfy social needs. Thanh Nien News.com. Accessed on July 14, 2008 at: *http://www.thanhniennews.com/commentaries/?catid=11&newsid= 19574*

43. VietnamNet Bridge, "Education for All?"

44. Mekong Private Sector Development Facility, "Provincial Economic Governance and Its Impact on Local Competitiveness."

45. Overland, "Higher Education Lags Behind the Times in Vietnam" and "Harvard Teaches Capitalism to Communists."

46. Boudreau, "Intel Reshaping Vietnam with a Billion-Dollar Chip-Assembly Plant."

47. World Bank, *Education in Vietnam*, pp. 22, 20 and passim.

48. VietnamNet Bridge, "University Boom Sparks Concerns About Quality."

49. Email to William Ratliff dated July 18, 2008.

Chapter 7

50. World Bank, *Vietnam Development Report 2006*, p. 59.

51. Vo Tri Thanh, *Managing Capital Flows*, pp. 6–8, quotes from pp. 9, 26, and 30.

Chapter 8

52. "Ministry of Finance: Loss-Making SOEs to Be Supervised," *Vietnam News Briefs.*

53. Tran Ngoc Phuong, *Reform of State Owned Enterprises in the Context of Vietnam's WTO Accession.*

54. Vietnam Business Finance, "SOEs Still the Mainstay of National Economy."

55. Asian Development Bank, *SOE Reform and Corporate Governance Facility.*

56. Vietnam Business Finance, "SOEs Still the Mainstay of National Economy."

57. Asia Pulse, "Vietnamese Conference to Accelerate State-Owned Privatisation."

58. Vo Tri Thanh, *Managing Capital Flows*, pp. 31, 38.

59. "Stock Market Vietinbank to Make IPO Late This Year," *Vietnam News Briefs.*

60. "Ministry of Finance: Loss-Making SOEs to Be Supervised," *Vietnam News Briefs.*

61. VietnamNet Bridge, "State Reports Solid Progress on SOE Equitisation Process."

62. "State Reluctance to Relinquish Control Hits Firms' Efficiency," *Thanh Nien News.*

Part III

Chapter 9

63. Kreft and Sobel, "Public Policy, Entrepreneurship, and Economic Freedom." See also Powell, *Making Poor Nations Rich.*
64. Gwartney and Lawson, *Economic Freedom of the World: 2006 Annual Report,* p. 5.
65. World Bank, *Doing Business 2007.*

Chapter 10

66. International Monetary Fund, Consultative Group Meeting for Vietnam. Statement by Shogo Ishii, assistant director, Asia and Pacific Development.
67. Mekong Private Sector Development Facility, *Beyond the Headline Numbers: Business Registration and Startup in Vietnam.*
68. Much of the information in this summary is taken from the World Bank's *Vietnam Development Report 2006,* pp. 3–6, and from General Statistics Office reports.
69. General Statistics Office of Vietnam, *Vietnam Household Living Standards Survey* (VHLSS), 2002, 2004: Basic Information. Retrieved on July 14, 2008 by Googling title.
70. World Bank, *Vietnam Development Report 2006,* p. 4.
71. How to minimize the risk of providing loans for SMEs, Communist Party of Vietnam Online Newspaper. December 17, 2007. Accessed on August 27, 2008, at *http://www .cpv.org.vn/details_e.asp?id=BT17120778434*

Chapter 11

72. Mekong Private Sector Development Facility. "Starting a Business in Vietnam: How Easy?" *Business Issues Bulletin,* August 2006.
73. See, for example, Mekong Private Sector Development Facility, *Beyond the Headline Numbers,* p. 45.
74. Mekong Private Sector Development Facility, *Beyond the Headline Numbers,* pp. 43, 10–13 and passim.
75. General Statistics Office of Vietnam, *The Real Situation of Enterprises Through the Preliminary Results of Survey Conducted in 2006.*
76. Mekong Private Sector Development Facility, *Beyond the Headline Numbers,* p. 44.

Chapter 12

77. World Bank, *Vietnam Development Report 2006* (VDR 2006).
78. General Statistics Office of Vietnam, *The Real Situation of Enterprises Through the Preliminary Results of Survey Conducted in 2006.* News reports on the GSO survey include *Vietnam Business Forum,* "97% Vietnam Businesses Are Small Scale"; and *Vietnam Investment Review,* "Private Firms Make Up Bulk of Business." Accessed on July 14, 2008 at: *http://www.gso.gov.vn/default_en.aspx?tabid=462&idmid=2,2&ItemID=5683*

79. World Bank, *VDR 2006,* pp. 12–14.
80. World Bank, *VDR 2006,* p. 20.
81. VietnamNet Bridge, "Conference Seeks Ways to Develop SMEs."
82. Cited in VDR 2006, p. 18. Vietnamnet Bridge, "National Strategy on Business Development Kick Started."
83. Mekong Private Sector Development Facility, "Private Sector Firms," *Business Issues Bulletin,* June 2005.
84. Mekong Private Sector Development Facility, "Effective Implementation: The next step for the new Enterprise and Investment Laws," *Business Issues Bulletin,* October 2006.
85. Mekong Private Sector Development Facility, "Doing Business in Vietnam: Policies improve in 2007 but obstacles remain," *Business Issues Bulletin,* October 2007.
86. Mekong Private Sector Development Facility, "Targeted Policies that Support Women's Entrepreneurship can Boost Vietnam's Economic Growth," *Business Issues Bulletin,* April 2006.
87. Mekong Private Sector Development Facility, *Women Business Owners in Vietnam: A National Survey* and, later, *Voices of Vietnamese Women Entrepreneurs.*
88. Central Institute for Economic Management, Danish Ministry of Foreign Affairs (Danida) Project, "Launching of Two Important Research Reports on Rural Household Living Conditions and SME Development."
89. The Return of the Boat People, Special Report: Vietnam, *The Economist,* April 24, 2008.
90. Ministry of Foreign Affairs, Vietnam. "Overseas Vietnamese, a Bridge Connecting Viet Nam and US." See also VietnamNet Bridge, "Administrative Reform to Boost Investment." Accessed on July 2, 2008 at: *http://www.mofa.gov.vn/en/nr040807104143/nr040807105001/ns05063010101018*
91. Boudreau, "Real Estate Rush: Silicon Valley Investors Join Market Frenzy in Ho Chi Minh City."

Part IV

Chapter 13

92. Two of the recent studies of land and land-related issues used in this section are Asian Development Bank, *The Impact of Land Market Processes on the Poor: Implementing de Soto;* and Mekong Private Sector Development Facility, *Beyond the Headline Numbers.*
93. Dao Trung Chinh and Vu Duy Thai, "Viewpoints: Limited Supply of Land," in Mekong Private Sector Development Facility, *Business Issues Bulletin,* April 2007. Accessed on August 27, 2008 by clicking "issue 22" at: http://www.ifc.org/ifcext/mekongpsdf.nsf/Content/Business_Issues_Bulletin
94. VDR 2006, p. 79.
95. On rural issues, see *Markets & Development Bulletin,* "Linking Farmers to Markets Through Contract Farming."
96. World Bank, *VDR 2006,* p. 81.
97. This problem of the absence of clear property titles, and the resulting dead capital, is

the focus of Hernando de Soto's book *The Mystery of Capital.*

98. Central Institute for Economic Management, "Launching of Two Important Research Reports."
99. Mekong Private Sector Development Facility, *Beyond the Headline Numbers,* p. 75.
100. See Mekong Private Sector Development Facility, *Beyond the Headline Numbers,* and Central Institute for Economic Management, "Agricultural Land Conversion for Industrial and Commercial Use." Agricultural Land Conversion for Industrial and Commercial Use, *Markets & Development Bulletin,* No. 8. Accessed July 14, 2008 at: *http://www.markets4poor.org/?name=publication&op=viewDetailNews&id=447*
101. See Mekong Private Sector Development Facility, *Beyond the Headline Numbers,* and Central Institute for Economic Management, "Agricultural Land Conversion for Industrial and Commercial Use." Agricultural Land Conversion for Industrial and Commercial Use, *Markets & Development Bulletin,* No. 8. Accessed July 14, 2008 at: *http://www.markets4poor.org/?name=publication&op=viewDetailNews&id=447*

Chapter 14

102. SME's wings clipped due to lack of capital. VietnamNet Bridge. Accessed July 14, 2008 at: *http://www.namdinhbusiness.gov.vn/News/tabid/318/TopicID/22/NewsID/46/Default. aspx*
103. Central Institute for Economic Management, "Launching of Two Important Research Reports."
104. Central Institute, "Launching."
105. World Bank, *Vietnam Development Report 2008,* Executive Summary and Chapter 5.
106. Mekong Private Sector Development Facility, *Beyond the Headline Numbers: Business Registration and Startup in Vietnam.* Private Sector Discussions, No. 20.

Chapter 15

107. See the Agency for SME Development website.
108. Mekong Private Sector Development Facility, *Vietnam: A Model for Improving the Local Business Environment.*

Chapter 16

109. Mekong Private Sector Development Facility, "Streamlining Business Licensing," June 2006.

Part V

Chapter 17

110. Christopher R. Hill. U.S.–Vietnam Bilateral Relations, State Department. Accessed on July 14, 2008 at: *http://www.state.gov/p/eap/rls/rm/2008/03/102143.htm.*

Chapter 18

111. See *SAWF News*, "Vietnam Must Clarify Laws and Fight Graft, Says Foreign Business," and Vietnam Business Forum, "Vietnam Business Forum 2006: More Improvement Needed."

112. Associated Press, "Vietnam Hails Imminent WTO Accession, Warns of Fierce Foreign Competition." For an excellent rundown on the basic issues involved in Vietnam's WTO entry, see Runckel and Associates, *What Impact Vietnam's New WTO Membership Will Have and What Vietnam Has Committed.*

113. Vietnam Ministry of Foreign Affairs. Outstanding Features of Foreign Direct Investments in Vietnam. Accessed on July 14, 2008 at: *http://www.mofa.gov.vn/en/tt_baochi/nr041126171753/ns071205095645.*

Part VI

114. Harvard Vietnam Program, *Choosing Success*, p. 3. The study cites Economist Intelligence Unit, *Vietnam: Country Forecast,* September 2007.

References

Abuza, Zachary. The Politics of Reform in Vietnam, 1986–2000. In *Vietnam: Current Issues and Historical Background,* edited by V. Largo, 1–22. New York: Nova Science Publishers, 2002.

———. Vietnam Today. *The History Place. http://www.historyplace.com/pointsofview/ vietnam.htm* (accessed December 2, 2006).

Agency for SME Development, Ministry of Planning and Investment. *SME Development Policy Guiding Principles.* Available at: *http://www.business.gov.vn/mastertop. aspx?LangType=1033* (accessed December 27, 2006).

Asian Development Bank. *Asian Development Outlook 2006.* Available at: *http://www .adb.org/documents/books/ado/2006/default.asp.*

———. *The Impact of Land Market Processes on the Poor: Implementing de Soto.* Discussion Paper no. 3 in the Making Markets Work Better for the Poor series, November 2004.

———. *Socialist Republic of Viet Nam: Strategic Secondary Education Planning and Cooperation.* 2006. Available at: *http://www.adb.org/* (accessed October 17, 2006).

———. *SOE Reform and Corporate Governance Facility.* September 6, 2006. Available at: *http://www.adb.org/Documents/Profiles/PPTA/39538012.ASP* (accessed October 28, 2006).

———. *Viet Nam.* Available at: *http://www.adb.org/Documents/Books/ADO/2008/VIE. pdf* (accessed May 29, 2008).

Asia Pulse. Vietnamese Conference to Accelerate State-Owned Privatisation, April 25, 2008.

Associated Press. Foreign Direct Investment in Vietnam Reaches US$15 Billion, More Than Double Last Year's Pace. *International Herald Tribune,* May 26, 2008. Available at: *http://www.iht.com/articles/ap/2008/05/26/business/AS-FIN-Vietnam-Foreign-Investment.php* (accessed July 14, 2008, click this link and then No. 8: *http://www. ifc.org/ifcext/mekongpsdf.nsf/Content/Market_Development_Bulletins*).

————. Silicon Valley Engineer Fights for Freedom, Democracy in Vietnam. October 23, 2006. Accessed on July 14, 2008 at: *http://www.iht.com/articles/ap/2006/10/23/america/NA_GEN_US_Vietnam_Freedom_Fighter.php.*

————. Vietnam Hails Imminent WTO Accession, Warns of Fierce Foreign Competition. *International Herald Tribune,* October 27, 2006. Available at: *http://www.iht.com/articles/ap/2006/10/27/business/AS_FIN_Vietnam_WTO.php* (accessed October 27, 2006).

Birdsall, Nancy, Dani Rodrik, and Arvind Subramanian. How to Help Poor Countries. *Foreign Affairs,* July/August 2005.

Bloomberg News. Around the Markets: Vietnam as Emerging China. *International Herald Tribune,* September 22, 2006. Available at: *http://www.iht.com/bin/print_ipub.php?file=/articles/2006/09/21/bloomberg/bxatm.php* (accessed October 29, 2006).

————. In Vietnam, Patience Pays Off. *International Herald Tribune,* October 26, 2006. Available at: *http://www.iht.com/bin/print_ipub.php?file=/articles/2006/10/25/bloomberg/bxfund.php* (accessed October 29, 2006).

Boudreau, John. Intel Reshaping Vietnam with a Billion-Dollar Chip-Assembly Plant. *San Jose Mercury News,* April 17, 2008.

————. Real Estate Rush: Silicon Valley Investors Join Market Frenzy in Ho Chi Minh City. *San Jose Mercury News,* May 30, 2008.

Bui Thi Bich Lien. Legal Education in Transitional Vietnam, in *Asian Socialism & Legal Change: The Dynamics of Vietnamese and Chinese Reform,* edited by John Gillespie and Pip Nicholson. Canberra: Asia Pacific Press at the Australian National University, 2005.

Buscaglia, Edgardo, and William Ratliff. *Law and Economics in Developing Countries.* Stanford: Hoover Institution Press, 2000.

Central Institute for Economic Management. Agricultural Land Conversion for Industrial and Commercial Use. *Markets & Development Bulletin,* April 2006. Accessed on July 14, 2008, click this link and then No. 8: *http://www.ifc.org/ifcext/mekongpsdf.nsf/Content/Market_Development_Bulletins*

Central Institute for Economic Management, Danish Ministry of Foreign Affairs (Danida) Project. Launching of Two Important Research Reports on Rural Household Living Conditions and SME Development. Available at: *http://www.ciem.org.vn/home/en/home/InfoDetail.jsp?area=1&cat=329&ID=1410* (accessed June 2, 2008).

China Daily. Hu Wraps Up US Visit with Yale Speech, April 21, 2006. Available at: *http://www.chinadaily.com.cn/china/2006–04/21/content_573942.htm* (accessed October 30, 2006).

Communist Party of Vietnam Online Newspaper, How to minimize the risk of providing loans for SMEs, Communist Party of Vietnam Online Newspaper. Accessed on August 27, 2008, at *http://www.cpv.org.vn/details_e.asp?id=BT1712077843*

_____. Objectives of International Economic Integration, May 28, 2003. Available at: *http://www.cpv.org.vn/details_e.asp?id=BT285039685* (accessed October 28, 2006).

Constitution of the Socialist Republic of Vietnam: 1992. Available at: *http://coombs.anu. edu.au/~vern/van_kien/constit.html* (accessed October 8, 2006).

de Soto, Hernando. *The Mystery of Capital: Why Capitalism Triumphs in the West and Fails Everywhere Else.* New York: Basic Books, 2000.

Economist. Special Report: Vietnam. April 24, 2008.

Fairbank, John King. *China: A New History.* Cambridge, MA: Belkap Press of Harvard University Press, 1992.

General Statistics Office of Vietnam. The Real Situation of Enterprises Through the Preliminary Results of Survey Conducted in 2006. December 2006. General Statistics URL, Accessed on August 27, 2008 at: *http://www.gso.gov.vn/default_en.aspx? tabid=462&idmid=2,2&ItemID=5683*

_____. Non-Farm Individual Business Establishment Survey, 2005. Available at: *http:// www.gso.gov.vn/default_en.aspx?tabid=480&idmid=4* (accessed on July 13, 2008 at: *http://www.gso.gov.vn/default_en.aspx?tabid=480&idmid=4&ItemID=4692*).

_____. *Vietnam Household Living Standards Survey, 2004.* Accessed on July 14, 2008 by Googling "Vietnam Household Living Standards Survey, 2004."

Gillespie, John. Changing Concepts of Socialist Law in Vietnam. In *Asian Socialism & Legal Change: The Dynamics of Vietnamese and Chinese Reform,* edited by John Gillespie and Pip Nicholson 45-75. Canberra: Asia Pacific Press at the Australian National University, 2005.

Gillespie, John, and Pip Nicholson, eds. *Asian Socialism & Legal Change: The Dynamics of Vietnamese and Chinese Reform.* Canberra: Asia Pacific Press at the Australian National University, 2005.

Gwartney, James, and Robert Lawson. *Economic Freedom of the World: 2006 Annual Report.* Vancouver, BC: The Fraser Institute, 2006. Available at: *http://www.freethe world.com/release.html* (accessed October 29, 2006).

Harrison, Lawrence. *The Central Liberal Truth: How Politics Can Change a Culture.* New York: Oxford University Press, 2006.

_____. Hearts, Minds, and Schools. *Washington Post,* December 17, 2006.

_____. *Underdevelopment Is a State of Mind: The Latin American Case.* Lanham, MD: Madison Books, 2000.

Harvard Vietnam Program, *Choosing Success: The Lessons of East and Southeast Asia and Vietnam's Future.* Harvard University, John F. Kennedy School of Government, Asia Programs, January 2008.

Heritage Foundation. *Index of Economic Freedom 2008.* Accessed on July 14, 2008 at: *http://www.heritage.org/research/features/index/countries.cfm* ; also: *http://www.heritage.org/research/features/index/countries.cfm*

Hoang Chi Bao. Socialist Democracy—Goal and Motivation of Renovation. *Communist Party of Vietnam Online Newspaper,* September 26, 2006. Available at: *http://www.cpv.org.vn/details_e.asp?id=BT2690659662*

International Monetary Fund. Consultative Group Meeting for Vietnam. Statement by Shogo Ishii, assistant director, Asia and Pacific Development, December 2007. Available at: *http://www.imf.org/external/np/dm/2007/121007.htm* (accessed June 2, 2008).

――――. IMF Country Report No. 06/421. IMF, Vietnam's New Challenges Amid Signs of Overheating. Accessed on July 14, 2008 at: *http://www.imf.org/external/pubs/ft/survey/so/2008/CAR03708A.htm*

――――. *Vietnam: Selected Issues.* IMF Country Report No. 06/422, November 2006.

Joiner, Alex. Examining the Vietnamese Dong. *Economics@ANZ,* August 2006. Australia and New Zealand Banking Group Limited. Available at: *www.anz.com/documents/economics/Vietnam_currency_update_Aug_2006.pdf*

Kreft, Steven, and Russell Sobel. Public Policy, Entrepreneurship, and Economic Freedom. *The Cato Journal,* Fall 2005. Available at: *http://www.cato.org/pubs/journal/cj25n3/cj25n3.html* (accessed October 29, 2006).

Lamb, David. *Vietnam, Now: A Reporter Returns.* New York: Public Affairs, 2002.

Mekong Private Sector Development Facility. *Beyond the Headline Numbers: Business Registration and Startup in Vietnam.* Private Sector Discussions no. 20, May 2005. Available at: *http://www.ifc.org/ifcext/mekongpsdf.nsf/Content/PSDP20* (accessed June 23, 2008).

――――. Doing Business In Vietnam: Policies improve in 2007 but obstacles remain, *Business Issues Bulletin,* October 2007. Accessed on August 27, 2008 by clicking Issue 25 at: *http://www.ifc.org/ifcext/mekongpsdf.nsf/Content/Business_Issues_Bulletin*

――――. Linking Farmers to Markets Through Contract Farming, *Markets & Development Bulletin.* March 2005. MPDF. Beyond the Headline Numbers, Accessed on July 14, 2008 at: *http://www.ifc.org/ifcext/mekongpsdf.nsf/Content/PSDP20.*

――――. Private Sector Firms, *Business Issues Bulletin,* June 2005.

――――. Provincial Economic Governance and Its Impact on Local Competitiveness. *Business Issues Bulletin* issue 26, March 2008. Accessed on July 14, 2008 at the following link, then click Issue 26: *http://www.ifc.org/ifcext/mekongpsdf.nsf/Content/Business_Issues_Bulletin*

――――. Starting a Business in Vietnam: How Easy? *Business Issues Bulletin,* no. 18, August 2006.

_____. Streamlining Business Licensing. *Business Issues Bulletin*, no. 17, June 2006.

_____. Targeted policies that support women's entrepreneurship can boost Vietnam's economic growth, *Business Issues Bulletin*, April 2006. Accessed on August 27, 2008 by clicking Issue 16 at: *http://www.ifc.org/ifcext/mekongpsdf.nsf/Content/Business_Issues_Bulletin*

_____. *Vietnam: A Model for Improving the Local Business Environment.* Available at: *http://www.ifc.org/ifcext/mekongpsdf.nsf/Content/Feature6* (accessed October 29, 2006).

_____. Viewpoints: Limited Supply of Land. *Business Issues Bulletin* no. 19, April 2007. Accessed on July 14, 2008 at the following link, then click Issue 22: *http://www.ifc .org/ifcext/mekongpsdf.nsf/Content/Business_Issues_Bulletin*

_____. *Voices of Vietnamese Women Entrepreneurs.* Hanoi, September 2006. Accessed on July 14, 2008 at: *http://www-wds.worldbank.org/servlet/main?menuPK=64187510 &pagePK=64193027&piPK=64187937&theSitePK=523679&entityID=000310607_ 20060929104723*

_____. *Women Business Owners in Vietnam: A National Survey.* Private Sector Discussions no. 21, March 2006. Available at: *http://www.ifc.org/ifcext/mekongpsdf.nsf/Content /PSDP21* (accessed June 25, 2008).

Ministry of Foreign Affairs, Vietnam. Outstanding Features of Foreign Direct Investments in Vietnam. Available at: *http://www.mofa.gov.vn/en/tt_baochi/nr041126171753/ ns071205095645* (accessed June 2, 2008).

_____. Overseas Vietnamese, a Bridge Connecting Viet Nam and US. Available at: *http://www.mofa.gov.vn/en/nr040807104143/nr040807105001/ns050630101018/view* (accessed June 2, 2008).

_____. Vietnam's Overseas Investment. Available at: *http://www.mofa.gov.vn/en/tt_ baochi/nr041126171753/ns071210082327/view* (accessed June 3, 2008).

Nguyen Khac Vien. *Vietnam: A Long History* (6th ed.). Hanoi: Gioi Publishers, 2004.

Nhan Dan. Vietnam Speeds Up Global Integration with Three More Laws. June 23, 2006. Accessed on July 14, 2008 at: *http://www.itpc.hochiminhcity.gov.vn/en/business_ news/business_day/2006/06/folder.2006−06−23.444534169/news_item.2006−06−23 .0562965941*

North, Douglass. *Institutions, Institutional Change and Economic Performance.* Cambridge: Cambridge University Press, 1990.

Overland, Martha Ann. Harvard Teaches Capitalism to Communists. *Chronicle of Higher Education,* June 9, 2006. Harvard Teaches Capitalism: Accessed on August 27, 2008 at: *http://chronicle.com/weekly/v52/i40/40a03801.htm*

_____. Higher Education Lags Behind the Times in Vietnam. *Chronicle of Higher Education,* June 9, 2006. Available at: Higher Ed Lags: Accessed on August 27, 2008 at: *http://chronicle.com/weekly/v52/i40/40a03601.htm*

Pham Duy Nghia. Confucianism and the Conception of the Law in Vietnam. In *Asian Socialism & Legal Change: The Dynamics of Vietnamese and Chinese Reform*, edited by John Gillespie and Pip Nicholson, 76–90. Canberra: Asia Pacific Press at the Australian National University, 2005.

Powell, Benjamin, ed. *Making Poor Nations Rich: Entrepreneurship and the Process of Economic Development*. Stanford, CA: Stanford University Press for the Independent Institute, 2008.

Ratliff, William. Confucianism + Capitalism = Economic Development. *Far Eastern Economic Review Forum*, December 2007. Accessed on July 14, 2008 at: *http://www.feer.com/economics/2008/february/Confucianism-Capitalism-Economic-Development*

Runckel and Associates. *What Impact Vietnam's New WTO Membership Will Have and What Vietnam Has Committed*. 2006. Accessed on August 27, 2008 at: *http://www.business-in-asia.com/wto_vietnam_impacts.html*

Saigon Times Weekly. Ambitious Generation Steps Forward. December 9, 2006. Available at: *http://www.saigontimesweekly.saigonnet.vn/data/focus_cover_story.htm* (accessed December 22, 2006).

San Jose Mercury News. Vietnam Tightens Grip on Internet. October 24, 2006.

SAWF News. Vietnam Must Clarify Laws and Fight Graft, Says Foreign Business. December 13, 2006. Accessed on July 14, 2008 at: *http://extendedremarks.blogspot.com/2006/12/vietnam-must-clarify-laws-and-fight.html*

St. George, Elizabeth. Socialist Ideology and Practical Realism: The Process of Compromise in Vietnam's Law on Education. In *Asian Socialism & Legal Change: The Dynamics of Vietnamese and Chinese Reform*, edited by John Gillespie and Pip Nicholson 115-134. Canberra: Asia Pacific Press at the Australian National University, 2005.

Tenev, Stoyan, Amanda Carlier, Omar Chaudry, and Quynh-Trang Nguyen. *Informality and the Playing Field in Vietnam's Business Sector*. Washington, DC: World Bank and International Finance Corp., 2003.

Thanh Nien News. State Reluctance to Relinquish Control Hits Firms' Efficiency. September 22, 2007. Available at: *http://www.thanhniennews.com/business/?catid=2&newsid=20367* (accessed May 31, 2008).

————. Vietnam's State Enterprise Too Much for Nothing. July 25, 2006. Available at: *http://www.thanhniennews.com/commentaries/?catid=11&newsid=18091* (accessed October 30, 2006).

Tran Ngoc Phuong. *Reform of State Owned Enterprises in the Context of Vietnam's WTO Accession*. Report delivered at Vietnam: Readiness for WTO Accession, organized by the National Center for Social Science and Humanity and the World Bank, June 2003, Hanoi and Ho Chi Minh City.

Trinh Quang Do. *Saigon to San Diego: Memoir of a Boy Who Escaped from Communist Vietnam*. Jefferson, NC: McFarland, 2004.

U.S. Commercial Service. *Doing Business in Vietnam: A Country Commercial Guide for U.S. Companies*. Washington: U.S. & Foreign Commercial Service, 2005. Accessed on July 14, 2008 at: *http://www.buyusa.gov/vietnam/en/country_commercial_guide. html*

U.S. State Department. *Background Note: Vietnam*. July 2006. Available at: *http://www .state.gov/r/pa/ei/bgn/4130.htm* (accessed October 29, 2006).

Vargas Llosa, Alvaro. *Liberty for Latin America: How to Undo Five Centuries of State Repression*. New York: Farrar, Straus and Giroux for the Independent Institute, 2005.

_____, ed. *Lessons from the Poor: Triumph of the Entrepreneurial Spirit*. Oakland, CA: The Independent Institute, 2008.

Vietnam Business Finance. SOEs Still the Mainstay of National Economy. April 23, 2008. Available at: *http://www.vnbusinessnews.com/2008/04/soes-still-mainstay-of-national-economy.html* (accessed May 31, 2008).

Vietnam Business Forum. 97% Vietnam Businesses Are Small Scale. December 8, 2006. Available at: *http://vibforum.vcci.com.vn/news_detail.asp?news_id=8417* (accessed December 26, 2006).

_____. Vietnam Business Forum 2006: More Improvement Needed. December 19, 2006. Accessed on August 27, 2008 at: *http://vibforum.vcci.com.vn/news_detail.asp? news_id=8507*

Vietnam Development Forum. *Vietnam as an Emerging Industrial Country: Policy Scope Toward 2020*, preview edition. Hanoi: Vietnam Development Forum, 2008. Available at: *http://www.vdf.org.vn/vdfreport.htm* (accessed June 1, 2008).

Vietnam Investment Review. Private Firms Make Up Bulk of Business. December 12, 2006. Available at: *http://www.vir.com.vn/Client/VIR/index.asp?url=content.asp& doc=12070* (accessed December 26, 2006).

Vietnam Ministry of Foreign Affairs. Outstanding Features of Foreign Direct Investment in Vietnam. Accessed on July 14, 2008 at: *http://www.mofa.gov.vn/en/nr040807104143/nr 040807105001/ns060908162838?b_start:int=15*

VietnamNet Bridge. Administrative Reform to Boost Investment. February 19, 2008. Available at: *http://english.vietnamnet.vn/biz/2008/02/769269/* (accessed June 2, 2008).

_____. Conference Seeks Ways to Develop SMEs. December 6, 2007. Available at: *http://english.vietnamnet.vn/biz/2007/12/758411/* (accessed June 2, 2008).

_____. Education for All? May 15, 2008. Accessed on July 14, 2008 at: *http://english. vietnamnet.vn/education/2008/05/783183/*

_____. Expert Discusses Problems of Vietnam's Education. May 14, 2008. Accessed on July 14, 2008 at: *http://english.vietnamnet.vn/education/2008/05/783067/*

————. National Strategy on Business Development Kick Started. October 13, 2006. Available at: *http://english.vietnamnet.vn/biz/2006/10/622230/* (accessed October 29, 2006).

————. State Reports Solid Progress on SOE Equitisation Process. September 22, 2006. Available at: *http://english.vietnamnet.vn/politics/2006/09/614807/* (accessed May 31, 2008).

————. University Boom Sparks Concerns About Quality. May 9, 2008. Accessed on July 14, 2008 at: *http://english.vietnamnet.vn/education/2008/05/782264/*

————. VND, to Float or Not to Float. Interview with Truong Van Phuoc. July 27, 2006. Accessed on August 27, 2008 at: *http://english.vietnamnet.vn/interviews/2005/07/472889/*

Vietnam News Briefs. Ministry of Finance: Loss-Making SOEs to Be Supervised. May 29, 2008.

————. Stock Market Vietinbank to Make IPO Late This Year. May 30, 2008.

Vo Tri Thanh and Pham Chi Quang. *Managing Capital Flows: The Case of Viet Nam*. Tokyo: ADB Institute, 2008. Available at: *http://www.adbi.org/discussion-paper/2008/05/16/2536.managing.capital.flows.vietnam/* (accessed June 19, 2008).

World Bank, *Doing Business 2008*. Accessed on August 27, 2008 at: *http://www.doing business.org/ExploreEconomies/?economyid=202*

————. *Education in Vietnam: Development History, Challenges and Solutions, 2006*. Washington, DC: World Bank. Accessed on August 27, 2008 by searching for title of document at: *http://www.worldbank.org*

————. *Taking Stock: An Update on Vietnam's Economic Developments and Reforms*. Accessed on August 27, 2008 by searching for title of document at: *http://www.world-bank.org*

————. *Vietnam Development Report 2006*. Accessed on August 27, 2008 by searching for the title of document at: *http://www.worldbank.org*

————. *Vietnam Development Report 2008: Social Protection*. Accessed on August 27, 2008 by searching for the title of document at: *http://www.worldbank.org*

World Economic Forum. *The Global Competitiveness Report 2007–2008*. Accessed on July 14, 2008 at: *http://www.weforum.org/en/initiatives/gcp/Global%20Competitiveness%20Report/index.htm*

Index

About the Author

WILLIAM RATLIFF is a Research Fellow at the Independent Institute and a member of the Board of Advisors of the Institute's Center on Global Prosperity. He is also a Research Fellow and Curator of the Americas Collection at the Hoover Institution, Stanford University. He received his Ph.D. in Latin American/Chinese history from the University of Washington.

Dr. Ratliff is author of *China's "Lessons" for Cuba's Transition, Russia's Oil in America's Future, Doing it Wrong and Doing it Right: Education in Latin America and Asia, The Law and Economics of Development* (with Edgardo Buscaglia), *A Strategic Flip-Flop in the Caribbean: Lift the Embargo on Cuba* (with Roger Fontaine), *Inside the Cuban Interior Ministry* (with Juan Antonio Rodriguez Menier), *The Civil War in Nicaragua: Inside the Sandinistas* (with Roger Miranda), *Castroism and Communism in Latin America*, and *The Soviet-Cuban Presence in East Africa*. He is contributing editor to *The Media and the Cuban Revolution* and coeditor of *Juan Peron: Cartas del exilio*. Dr. Ratliff was Latin American editor of the *Yearbook on International Communist Affairs*, a contributor to the annual *Latin America and Caribbean Contemporary Record*, and book review editor of the *Journal of Interamerican Studies and World Affairs*.

His articles have appeared in the *Wall Street Journal, New York Times, Chicago Tribune, Washington Post*, the *Los Angeles Times, International Herald Tribune, El Mercurio* (Santiago), *Globe and Mail* (Toronto), and *South China Morning Post* (Hong Kong). He has written for the MSNBC "Opinion" section and contributed to the award-winning Panama hand-over section of the on-line NewsHour with Jim Lehrer. He has been interviewed on CNN, NPR, PBS, APR, BBC, Voice of America, Radio Marti, and many other radio and TV stations around the world.

He has taught at Stanford University, San Francisco State University, University of San Francisco, Tunghai University in Taiwan, Diplomatic Academy at Lake Tahoe and other universities; monitored elections in El Salvador, Costa Rica, and Chile; and conducted private lecture tours in Latin America, China, and Southeast Asia.

INDEPENDENT STUDIES IN POLITICAL ECONOMY

For further information and a catalog of publications, please contact:
THE INDEPENDENT INSTITUTE
100 Swan Way, Oakland, California 94621-1428, U.S.A.
510-632-1366 · Fax 510-568-6040 · info@independent.org · www.independent.org